LOVE LIES BLEEDING

Also by Trevor Stammers

The Family Guide to Sex and Intimacy

Also in this series

Pills, Poppers and Caffeine
Addiction and Your Family
by David Partington

Laid Bare
A Path through the Pornography Maze
by Claire Wilson-Thomas and Nigel Williams

Love Lies Bleeding

When Intimacy Turns to Abuse

Trevor Stammers

Hodder & Stoughton

LONDON SYDNEY AUCKLAND

British Library Cataloguing in Publication Data
A record for this book is available from the British Library

ISBN 0 340 63043 4

Printed and bound in Great Britain by
Cox & Wyman, Reading, Berks.

Hodder and Stoughton Ltd
A Division of Hodder Headline PLC
338 Euston Road
London NW1 3BH

To Mary,
who came through the fire and rain,
and to
Barbara, Margaret and Peggy,
who help others to come through

Contents

Acknowledgments

Barbara and Les Davidson have both been invaluable in arranging interviews and providing many helpful insights in our discussions together.

Edward George and his assistants Marco and Jen at the Hirson Library, St Helier Hospital, Carshalton, have once again provided me with hundreds of pages of research data.

Elspeth Taylor, my editor, has been a model of both encouragement and patience over the past year.

Most important, my wife Rachel and my children Matthew, Laura and Elliot have for the second time sacrificially given of themselves in order to free me to write. In spite of this, our own love does not lie bleeding. I marvel at its durability, and thank God for it.

I express my indebtedness to all the above and to the many courageous people who have shared their experiences with me and whose stories appear in this book.

Trevor Stammers, 1996

Preface

Domestic violence is a brutal business, and it should be everyone's business. One quarter of all violent incidents reported to the police are episodes of domestic violence,[1] and it has been estimated that only 2 per cent of such episodes are reported in the first place.[2] So it's a common problem – but even more commonly ignored. The book draws attention to domestic violence as a pressing social issue. It will offer practical help and understanding to those suffering abuse at the hands of their intimate partners. Violent men who want to change will also find much useful material here.

But I aim to inform and challenge others too – parents, teachers, social workers, church leaders, legal and health-care professionals, as well as relatives, friends and neighbours.

We'll look at how domestic violence remains hidden, what makes men assault their partners and what effects the violence has on women and children. We'll consider the difficulties women face in coping with, and escaping from, violent relationships and the help (or lack of it) available to them. Finally the prevention of domestic violence will be explored.

Sadly, the home is often the venue for other types of abuse, such as abuse towards children and the elderly, but I have restricted my focus here to violence between intimate partners. The vast majority of such violence is perpetrated by men, and this book emphasises this imbalance repeatedly. The topical issue of battered men is, however, debated in chapter 7.

Choice of language is always important in discussing any issues relating to sex and gender. I recently attended a conference on domestic violence where the use of nearly every term was hotly disputed: 'Fish are battered – women are assaulted.' 'The use of the term "victim" is to be avoided, as it implies passivity and helplessness.'

I am acutely aware of these potential difficulties, but for the sake of brevity I have had to make a choice of words without qualifying them all. My aim throughout is to highlight the plight of the many women who live with – and sometimes die as a result of – domestic violence, and to explore what we can all do to end their nightmare.

1

Home is Where the Hurt Hides

Why Domestic Violence
Goes Undetected

Charity and beating begins at home.

John Fletcher

When I married Tim, I thought we'd have a wonderfully happy life together, just like my parents. Never in my wildest dreams did I imagine that I'd ever feel such terror, such absolute terror, of the man I loved. When it was at its worst, I would just lie there helplessly on the floor while he pummelled me for what seemed like an eternity. I often wondered if I'd ever get up or be able to walk again. Tell them about people like me. They need to know out there. It could just as easily happen to them, and it may already be happening to a relative, friend or neighbour.

The earnestness shone from Julia's eyes as she spoke. Yet as I looked around her spacious beautifully furnished home, it was hard to believe that she had been so savagely beaten and abused within its lavish walls for fifteen years – and during all that time nobody else knew anything about it.

There are people like Julia all around us – in our places of work, our parks, our pubs, our clubs and even in our churches, synagogues, mosques and temples. It's a myth that domestic violence is only a problem in someone else's neighbourhood. It may be easier to hide from public view within the fenced acres around a six-bedroom mansion, but it's still there and every bit as terrifying as when the screams are all too easily heard each night through the paper-thin walls of the tenement block.

An iceberg of terror

Domestic violence has always existed from ancient times. A team of palaeopathologists from the Medical College of Virginia identified a much higher incidence of fractures (30–40 per cent) in women than in men (9–20 per cent) in several finds of mummies dated as 2,000–3,000 years old.[1] These fractures were mostly of the skull and caused by interpersonal violence in peacetime. Many of them were doubtless the result of spouse abuse.

The Roman emperor Nero kicked his second wife, Poppaea Sabina, to death while she was pregnant just because she had criticised him for being back late from the races. (I suspect, however, that they had considerable marital discord prior to this final parting.)

Old English common laws, which were also adopted in America, permitted wife-beating for the purpose of correcting behaviour deemed inappropriate by husbands. One such law, in effect right up to the end of the nineteenth century, allowed men to beat their wives with a stick – as long as they didn't use one any thicker than their thumb. This is the origin of the phrase 'rule of thumb'. During the research for this book several men in their seventies told me they remembered seeing their own grandmothers being beaten by their husbands.

The current statistics are both alarming and getting worse.

In the UK there are estimated to be around half a million assaults on women by their partners each year.[2] This means that some 750,000 children are growing up in an atmosphere of hatred and fear as a result of such attacks on their mothers. In the USA between 8 million and 12 million women are at risk of physical abuse by their current intimate partner.[3] Around 1.5 million to 2 million are actually beaten each year – a rate of one every eighteen seconds.[4]

Not surprisingly, the exact incidence of wife-battering is difficult to be sure about, however. No official statistics are kept, and the number of incidents that are reported to the police is bound to be an underestimate. I frequently see women whose injuries have obviously resulted from an attack, yet they tell me that they have fallen over in the garden or offer other similarly unconvincing explanations.

The centre for criminology at Middlesex University recently reported a survey in which six out of ten men interviewed saw violence against their partner as a possible option. One in five men had struck their partner at least once in the previous year. The survey estimated that as many as one in ten women are victims of repeated domestic violence.[5]

How is it that something which occurs so frequently often remains totally unnoticed? I would suggest that this tendency to blind spots is by no means restricted to domestic violence. A few years ago I was researching into a viral infection called roseola infantum. This condition is generally accepted as the most common viral infection of infancy. Virtually all children have had it by the age of two years, yet most parents (and, I suspect, many doctors) have never even heard of it. It gives rise to a very high fever for several days, and later on a characteristic rash develops. If the condition is unknown to parent or doctor, it will, of course, go unrecognised and be labelled as measles or something else even though its features are quite different.

The same is true of domestic violence: ignorance of its frequency, an insufficiently low threshold of suspicion about its possible presence and lack of awareness of its multiple forms and features may result in failure to detect it. Let's look at some of the many faces of domestic violence that enable it to hide so well in the crowd.

Verbal abuse

The old adage 'Sticks and stones may break my bones but words will never hurt me' wears pretty thin with most victims of domestic violence. Nearly all suffer cruel verbal abuse from their partners. This can range from being called 'useless' or 'stupid' two or three times a week to a daily torrent of blasphemy and swearing.

> *He'd regularly call me a silly bitch or a whore in front of our five-year-old daughter and then go on to tell me how pathetic I was as a wife and how he didn't know why he put up with me.*

It is easy to see how verbal abuse undermines the self-esteem of the victim, but it is perhaps less easy to appreciate how it may predispose a person to violence. Most people swear and curse only when provoked or when things go badly wrong. The use of an expletive is, for these people, a release of violent emotion in itself. It is exceptional for them to use words as instruments of violent expression in this way.

When the use of expletives and four-letter words is normalised through constant repetition in daily life, however, there can be no recourse to cursing and verbal abuse to express anger and frustration in situations of real stress and provocation. The verbal reserve is already used up, and physical violence is more likely. I have yet to meet a batterer who did not use widespread verbal abuse routinely.

Verbal abuse of a partner may also have unintended harmful effects upon children. For years as a small boy Winston overheard his mother screaming and yelling at his father and telling him what a 'bumbling idiot and useless clod' he was. His father tried to ignore her quietly as best he could. Neither parent recognised the damage this was doing to Winston. He gradually lost all respect for his father and grew to hate his mother. Home was hell, so when the first taste of 'heaven' was offered by the drug-pushers at his school, Winston thought, 'Why not?' Smoking that first joint was the initial step for Winston on a downward spiral into drug addiction. Being stoned killed the pain of life at home – at least for a few precious hours.

Humiliation

This technique of control and domination is often expressed verbally, by making belittling comments about a partner in front of friends, for instance. Boasting about real or fabricated sexual conquests and making cruel comparisons is another common example. But humiliation can take many non-verbal forms.

> *He would make me get down on my hands and knees and scrub the house from top to bottom before sending me out to dig the garden. If he found I'd missed one weed, he'd force my head down and rub my face in it. He'd even take out a ruler to check that the edge of the lawn was straight. If it wasn't, the ruler would come down across the back of my skull.*

One particularly striking example of humiliation that sticks in my mind was provided by a girl who couldn't believe that she was going to sleep in a real bed when she sought help at the Women's Aid refuge where my practice provides medical care. For years her husband had made her sleep on the floor under the bed (just like a child's potty) because he was dissatisfied with her performance in the bed.

Conjugal terrorism

For some women, life at home bears more resemblance to that of a hostage rather than a wife or partner – indeed, their existence has been dubbed 'conjugal terrorism'. The destruction of favourite items or the fabric of the home and the restriction of both personal and financial liberty are common forms of abuse of power in such cases of domestic violence.

> *He would always lock me in the house and unplug the telephone and take it with him whenever he wasn't there. On one occasion he locked me in the understairs cupboard all evening. That was terrifying – supposing the house had caught fire or he had had an accident while he was out and no one knew I was there? The only times I was allowed out were twice a week to do the shopping, and if I wasn't back within an hour, he would interrogate me for hours afterwards and then insist on searching me to make sure I wasn't hiding anything from him. All my mail was opened and vetted before I was allowed to read it, and, needless to say, all the money was in his account. He kept control of the lot and only gave me just about enough to meet the weekly shopping bill.*

Monica's married life with Harley turned into a nightmare of suspicion. He went away on business one weekend, leaving her alone with their little girl, Susie. On the Saturday night, after putting Susie to bed, Monica went up to have a bath. When she opened the airing cupboard to get a fresh towel, she screamed in terror as the man inside stepped out. It was Harley. He had been hiding there all day, suspecting that

Monica was having an affair that he was bound to find out about by hiding in the house all weekend.

Physical abuse

This is what most commonly springs to mind when domestic violence is mentioned, yet even here patterns of abuse vary widely. Punches and kicks may be accompanied by other violent attacks, ranging from beatings with a hammer to scalding water being poured over the victim.

Violence like this can result in injuries, from black eyes and cuts right through to major burns and fractures. Internal damage, especially to the kidneys and lungs, can also easily occur. Pregnancy is an event which often either precipitates violence for the first time or else accelerates previously existing violence. In such circumstances being beaten can cause antenatal bleeding, threatened or actual miscarriage, premature labour or even loss of the baby through an intra-uterine death.

Some abusers will ensure that injury is never caused to the face of their victim so that detection of their activities will be more difficult. Typically attacks occur behind closed doors, but I know of at least one woman whose husband usually beat her up in public, though he never did it near their home or anywhere that they were likely to be recognised.

Sexual abuse

One of the saddest of all paradoxes is that sexual intercourse, perhaps the most powerful means of communicating marital love, can also turn into a hideous form of power abuse, marital rape. Several separate research studies have shown that around 10 per cent of married women surveyed in both the UK and the USA said that their husbands had tried to have sex with them by using physical force or the threat of it.[6]

One of my patients who had severe vaginal dryness with resultant bleeding told me that her husband had consequently hurt her during intercourse for years. She endured it silently, feeling that she had to accede to his desires and thinking that she was abnormal in not particularly wanting sex. She also confessed that he hit her on a fairly regular basis but that she felt this also was just 'normal married life'.

Murder

Many women have told me that they thought they were going to die as they felt their partner's fingers tighten around their throat or saw the glint of the knife-blade in his hand as he moved towards them. Often they have escaped death only by seconds.

Strangulation is particularly common; it is quiet and, with practice, need not leave any bruising. Abusive men get plenty of practice. Many develop the technique of strangling their wives into an art form – knowing just when to release the deadly grip as she loses consciousness so that she survives. But the next time she may not be so lucky.

Killing a spouse is the extreme end of a whole spectrum of domestic violence, and the difference between murder and physical abuse may simply be the thickness of the victim's skull or the angle of the blow that is struck. As it is, about 40 per cent of all murders of women in the UK involve men killing their partner or wife.[7] In the light of such statistics, 'til death us do part' takes on a whole new meaning.

What is it that drives men to curse, demean, terrorise, mutilate, rape and even murder their intimate partners? That is the subject of the next chapter.

2

Prone to Violence

Why Do Men Abuse Their Partners?

There's supposed to be a fine line between aggression and violence. Let's just say that geography wasn't my strong point!

Gareth Chilcott

One thing soon becomes very clear in any discussion about what makes men turn violent – there are no simple answers. A vast array of both social and personal factors contribute to violence in individual cases, and they often overlap. For example, society's general acceptance of heavy drinking may encourage a man under specific personal stress to have 'one too many', lose control and hit his wife.

Bearing in mind such interactions between causes, let us look at some of the major factors that lead to domestic violence.

Dad showed me how

Robert was brought up in India. His father was a tea planter there and a well-known and respected figure in the expatriate community. The family lived on a large estate and had two luxurious holiday flats on the coast. But there was trouble in paradise.

Father was very violent towards my mother, and we were regularly caned and beaten ourselves. You could always hear when Mum was getting it. I'd just disappear to my room. It hurt me so much to watch the father I loved doing that to her. I remember when I was five or six, we were staying in one of the flats. It had a beautiful polished wooden floor and there were lots of large flowerpots filled with tropical shrubs. I can still hear the sound of those pots breaking as he threw my mother around the room. She was screaming and screaming. Then later, when it was all over, I crept down; there was dirt and shattered fragments of pottery everywhere, and my mother huddled in a corner, groaning and sobbing bitterly. I knew that wasn't the way to treat a woman, but as I grew up it was easy to do it because my father did it.

The idea that violence begets violence makes intuitive sense and is borne out by many painful stories like Robert's. Indeed, this concept of what social scientists call the **intergenerational transmission of violence** is firmly established in the public consciousness. There is strong scientific evidence to support it too. An expert on domestic violence, Richard Gelles, confirms that 'One of the consistent conclusions of domestic-violence research is that individuals who have experienced violent and abusive childhoods are more likely to grow up and become child- and spouse-abusers than those with no experience of violence',[1] though it is witnessing violent attacks on their mothers, rather than being physically abused themselves as children, that is more generally associated with boys becoming spouse-abusers in adulthood. In some studies as many as two thirds of men who hit their partners had witnessed their father's violence towards their mother.[2]

Just as being abused as a child leads to an increased chance that a man or woman will become a child-abuser, so being a witness to the violent abuse of their mother places boys at greater risk of becoming batterers and girls at greater risk of becoming victims of battering. A modelling process takes place in which boys learn to express themselves by lashing out and girls develop a tolerance to violence which inhibits them from resisting it. Sometimes violence is the only means that some children experience of gaining their parents' attention. One young girl in the Woman's Aid refuge that my medical practice covers ran up to her mother shouting, 'Hit me, mummy, hit me.' Observing the refuge manager's raised eyebrows, the mother wryly commented, 'Don't worry. It's the way we show love in our family.'

Not all children who grow up in violent homes become violent themselves, however. There are protective factors which make some children less vulnerable than others in this regard. It is also worth noting that there is no convincing evidence to indicate that smacking a child within the context of a genuinely loving, caring family will predispose that child to violent behaviour in later life. Indeed, Henry Kempe, one of the first doctors to draw attention to the existence of child abuse, defined it by saying, 'Child abuse is the difference between a hand on the bottom and a fist in the face.'[3]

One of the problems of drawing conclusions about cause and effect when looking at studies of children who have witnessed parental violence at home is that genetic factors may be involved.

There is currently a resurgence of interest in the association between our genetic make-up and our predisposition to criminality, including violent behaviour. One resident on Death Row in the USA has appealed against his conviction on the grounds that he couldn't help killing because of his genetic pre-programming!

There almost certainly are genetic factors predisposing people to violence. It has been known for a long time that there is a hereditary element involved in, for example, alcohol abuse, which, as we shall see, is in itself a common accompaniment to spouse battery. But having a genetic 'fault' is a far cry from claiming it's not our fault, and the debate about responsibility for our actions in relation to our genetic make-up is essentially no different for domestic violence than for other areas.

Alcohol and drugs

As he came down the stairs I could see that he was a hard man. Not a flicker of emotion in his face. Staring granite eyes, unshaven, alcohol on his breath and a waxy redness in his cheeks.

It was his wife who really startled me, though. She worked on the cosmetics counter at a well-known London store. Immaculately made-up and smartly dressed, she always made a good impression on her customers. Now she looked more like a hag from *Macbeth*. Tousled, dowdy hair, bloodshot eyes filled with tears, wrinkled dry skin, a bleeding lip and barely able to speak. The cause of the riches-to-rags transformation was plain enough. They'd both got drunk, and he'd beaten the living daylights out of her again.

Alcohol abuse is a common antecedent of domestic violence – over half the battered wives in one study said their husbands got drunk every week[4] – but the role played by alcohol varies.

When intoxicated, men who drink too much are likely to be prone to violence towards their spouses, but in addition their alcohol misuse will probably lead to complications which may trigger violent attacks even when they are not actually drunk.

Alcohol impairs co-ordination, so falls and injuries are probable, and when they occur the abuser may take it out on his partner when he recovers. Breakages of household furniture and personal possessions may lead to outbursts of rage.

Wasting of the testes and weak erections are other complications of alcohol excess, and sexual frustration may trigger the battering of a partner.

A compounding problem is that many women will themselves turn to drink for relief when they are assaulted. This tends to make them more aggressive in turn, thus precipitating further attacks by their partners.

The academic debate about whether men drink deliberately in order to have an excuse for their violent attacks or whether a problem with drinking leads them to become violent is of little relevance to their partners, who are injured badly whatever the primary cause.

Though alcohol is the abused substance most commonly associated with domestic violence, drug abuse is also related. Drugs such as heroin, ecstasy and crack are allied to increased levels of aggression. There is also anecdotal evidence linking the use of steroids for body-building with an increase in the incidence of spouse battering.[5]

Power play

I've felt vulnerable all my life. I was trying to exert power over [women] so that I was in control and they felt vulnerable.

It was Bertrand Russell who suggested that 'the fundamental concept in social science is Power, in the same sense that in which Energy is the fundamental concept in Physics'.[6] The problem is that power in social terms is generally difficult to define and measure. Marital power is no exception.

A useful concept in discussing power conflict in marriage is that of **power bases**, which are defined as personal assets, such as knowledge, skill, insight and financial resources, that form the foundation of one partner's control over the other.

Power bases also include the cultural norms relating to the issue of who has the authority in a relationship. Historically it has been considered a normal part of married life for a husband to control his wife, using physical force if necessary, and that attitude still constitutes part of the macho image which many men feel they have to project.

Patriarchal attitudes are also greatly influenced by religious and spiritual beliefs. In the Christian tradition, for example, some of the early Church fathers wrote very disparagingly about women. St John Chrysostom described women as 'weak and fickle',[7] and Thomas Aquinas wrote, 'The particular nature of the active male seed intends to produce a perfect likeness of itself, and when females are conceived this is due to weak seed or unsuitable material or external influences like the dampness of the south wind.'[8] Some of St Paul's letters in the New Testament also contain a few passages which, particularly when read in the Authorised Version, seem to belittle the role and status of women. However, it is clear from the Acts of the Apostles that Paul, like Jesus before him, greatly valued the friendship of women, and his more controversial statements about the role of women are open to more than one interpretation (see pp. 36–7). Yet old prejudices die hard, and there is still an undeniable problem of spouse-abuse within Christian communities in Britain.[9] The extent of the problem in the USA is detailed by James and Phyllis Alsdurf in their book *Battered Into Submission*,[10] which paints a grim picture of the harsh, authoritarian domination of their families by some Christian husbands, who readily use violence to force their will on their wives and children and see this to be the will of God.

Christianity is not alone in this regard. Within Islam, for example, there is also a patriarchal power system which tends to promote and perpetuate violence against women. The Koran expressly states:

14

> *Men have authority over women because God has made the one superior to the others, and because they spend their wealth to maintain them. Good women are obedient. They guard their unseen parts because God has guarded them. As for those from whom you fear disobedience, admonish them and send them to beds apart and beat them. Then if they obey you, take no further action against them.*[11]

Because in Islamic cultures religion and law are one, such teaching is not only a religious duty but a legal right. However, even in Saudi Arabia, possibly one of the most conservative societies in the world, the law now places considerable limitations on the amount of physical punishment a husband may inflict on his wife.

Of course, not every man within either a religious or a secular patriarchal culture will beat his partner, and there are many other personal power bases which come into play in determining whether violent behaviour will erupt. A woman whose occupation has a higher status than her husband's job is much more likely to experience violent attacks at home; when the man's job is higher in status, there is less likelihood of domestic violence. Similarly, if a woman is better educated than her partner, the risk of violence is increased, and the same applies if her income is greater than her partner's. Control of money, as we have seen (p. 6), is a frequent means of exercising domination, and it is no surprise that among couples who share a joint account there is a lower incidence of wife battery.

Poor communication skills are another factor associated with battering by men. Assaultive men have a strong desire for power, yet lack the verbal resources to achieve control in an intimate relationship. The only means of communication they can call on is violence.

Patriarchal power play, then, is clearly an important factor in the development of violence in the home. In partnerships where the man dominates the decision-making, wife battering is about six to eight times more likely than in egalitarian marriages.[12]

Family structure and home as a hideaway

We believe that the institution of marriage, which by centuries-long tradition gives husbands the right to rule 'their' households, encourages men to abuse their power over women and children.
Ann Jones and Susan Schechter, *When Love Goes Wrong*[13]

Many people believe that marriage is at least partly to blame for encouraging partner abuse. This view is entirely understandable, but the real problem is that marriage has a long history of being abused itself. The concept of a woman being her husband's chattel is not an intrinsic part of marriage, nor is such a concept unique to marriage. It is deplorable that right up until 1878 the law in Britain regarded a wife as part of her husband's property, and she could, for example, be forcibly detained in the man's home. Marriage does not need such misguided laws to 'uphold' it, and marriage today tends to act as a protection against domestic violence.

Some of the evidence for this is indirect. For example, in about a third of families where partner-battery occurs, physical child-abuse also takes place,[14] and in up to 40 per cent of child-abuse cases, battering of the child's mother is going on as well.[15] Robert Whelan, in his book *Broken Homes and Battered Children*,[16] gives a detailed analysis of recent national statistics, showing that children living with two cohabiting natural parents are twenty times more at risk of being battered than children living with two married natural parents. Given the high association of child-battering with violence between

16

parents, this suggests that partner-abuse is also more likely among cohabitees.

Direct confirmation of this is provided by studies which have shown that marriage is associated with a lower risk of battering and that overall cohabitees are more violent than married couples.[17] Other research has shown that in over half of the wife-battery cases surveyed the violence had begun long before marriage, and marriage did not increase the rate of violent incidents.[18]

Reconstituted families in which children have been fathered by previous partners form another high-risk group.[19] Stepchildren are frequently a source of marital conflict and are themselves at much greater than average risk of being abused or murdered by a parent. A batterer is typically an over-possessive and jealous man who resents his predecessor's children as living reminders of his incomplete monopoly over his wife. He often wreaks his revenge on wife and children alike.

Irrespective of the family structure within it, the private nature of the home means that there are fewer social constraints on behaviour within its four walls than outside. This privacy makes wife-battering easy to commit and unlikely to be detected and reprimanded. In fact, it has been calculated that a batterer has a 99.62 per cent chance of *never* being punished by the courts.

Personality traits

Men who are violent to their partners tend to have personality characteristics which predispose them to coping poorly with stress in their relationships. Though there is no single psychological profile that fits every batterer, most such men show:

- insecurity
- low self-esteem

- poor verbal communication
- manipulative behaviour
- dominating tendencies
- obsessional jealousy
- lack of personal assertiveness skills
- Jekyll-and-Hyde personalities.

These traits are vividly illustrated by women who have been the victims of such men.

> *He said that he would ditch me if I ever went to college.*

> *I worked in the local library and he would come and spy on me. If I talked to men at the check-out desk, I was flirting. If I put books on the shelf and my legs showed, I was being provocative to other men. He was continually jealous and would see sex in everything I did.*

> *It was terrifying. I never knew what to expect next. One minute we'd be laughing and joking together over a bottle of wine, and the next he'd be at my throat with a knife.*

Mental illness

In men suffering from psychotic conditions such as acute schizophrenia and mania, violence is much more likely than in mentally healthy men, since the perpetrator literally doesn't know what he's doing. Most domestic violence is not linked with madness, however.

With other psychiatric conditions associated with battering, it can be difficult to distinguish between cause and effect in both the aggressors and their victims. For example, many men who batter are found to be clinically depressed when they are assessed during treatment programmes to control their violence, but this may be a secondary reaction, as they come to terms with what they have done, rather than a condition predisposing them to the original violence.

Poverty and unemployment

Poor housing, overcrowding, low income and debt are stress-provoking situations which may precipitate episodes of domestic violence where other factors make violence a probable pattern of behaviour, but they are unlikely to be primary factors. Certainly, in our local Woman's Aid centre we have come to recognise the increasing frequency of what the manager has dubbed the 'designer-curtain syndrome', where a battered woman arrives on the doorstep clutching the camcorder, CD player and video!

Pornography and social acceptance

The general acceptance in society of the macho image of masculinity encourages both violent behaviour and the use of pornography on the grounds that 'boys will be boys'.

Boys may be batterers, however, if they are exposed to pornography without any protective counterbalances in their lives. Because pornography is usually consumed alone, the message conveyed by it is neither discussed nor contradicted – a message, most commonly, about using women and children in the sexual service of men.

> *The more videos he saw, the more he wanted me to do the things he saw in them. I became so anxious that eventually I couldn't perform in bed at all. That was when he started to hit me.*

In one study 39 per cent of battered women (but only 3 per cent of non-battered women) had been asked by their partners to re-enact pornographic materials.[20] Other research has indicated that between 40 and 50 per cent of batterers regularly use pornographic magazines, films and videos.[21]

I once took part in a *Cook Report* programme on pornography. During the programme I was shown some examples of recent pornographic computer images. As I looked at these pictures of sexual parts, rather than of women, they reminded me of carcasses of meat on a butcher's slab. If they conjured up thoughts of slaughter in me as a doctor, I wondered what sorts of violent ideas they would arouse in those without the checks and balances that my background and training have instilled in me.

The violence within

I have lived and worked for over a decade in what most people would regard as a quiet, well-heeled part of London, yet in that time there have been several murders within a mile or so of my practice, and violent incidents are so common that they are part of my everyday work. Evil is an undeniable reality among my patients, and I recognise its power in myself too. I have never struck my wife, but I have verbally and emotionally abused her on rare occasions, sometimes without recognising it. The potential for evil lies within us all and often expresses itself violently. Well-brought-up, decent, respectable people, normally quiet as doves, can suddenly break out in the most unexpected brutality.

In his book *The Violence Within* the psychiatrist Paul Tournier describes, with disarming candour, how he once hit his wife. He concludes, 'It is not a case of there being two camps, the camp of the violent and the camp of the non-violent, however hard the latter try to hide their violence.'[22] We are all in the same camp, and need to find appropriate ways to deal with our inner tendency to violence. This includes women too, as we shall see in chapter 7.

Possibilities, not certainties

I have discussed a number of predisposing factors and triggers of wife-battering. These could conveniently be classified in three main groups:

- the personality and background of the batterer
- the relationship between partners
- the social environment.

I have made no attempt to categorise them formally in this way, though, because there is so much interaction between the groups of triggers. Some factors lead to violence more directly than others – for example unemployment is a more indirect cause than marital conflict – but a man with an alcohol-abusing past may hit the bottle in order to try to cope with the frustration of unemployment. His drinking may then lead to higher levels of marital conflict, resulting in violence.

Many similar pathways to violence are easy enough to envisage, but it is important to realise they represent only possibilities or trends, not certainties. The origins of domestic violence are complex, and it is a mistake to think about them in too simple a fashion. Consider, for instance, the case of the young boy who sees his mother being beaten. He rushes to defend her and holds up his arms, shouting, 'No, Daddy, no! Don't hit her!' That boy, instead of imitating his father and becoming an abuser himself in adult life, may grow up to become a victim of battering. Having never known a woman in any role other than that of someone who is weak and in need of defence, he could become easy prey to a controlling and ultimately violent wife, or he could emotionally smother a normally placid woman so intensely that she eventually strikes out at him.

21

Explanations, not excuses

After this review of just some of the reasons why men batter their intimate partners, I must emphasise that *none of these reasons excuses violent behaviour*. In spite of their witnessing of parental violence, their exposure to pornography, their patriarchal upbringing, their poverty, their illness and their innate capacity for violence, most men do not hit their wives. The man who does has ultimately chosen to do so. This fact makes him responsible for his violence and means he should suffer the consequences, but it also offers him the potential for change, as we shall see.

Having looked at a wide range of behaviours used by abusive men and some of the factors that make them act this way, we will consider in the next chapter the devastating effects abuse has on women.

3

Battered Into Submission

The Effects of Domestic Violence

What good fortune for those in power that people do not think.

Adolf Hitler

Some of the physical effects of assault are obvious to see and can be quick to heal – five days at most for a cut on the face. The physical effects of battery do not stop with the immediate injuries, however. Long-term problems can ensue from which the recovery process is often slow and difficult. Symptoms as various as headaches, tiredness, muscle cramps and weakness, insomnia, nightmares, nausea and vomiting, anorexia, rashes, tremors, painful periods, irritable bowel syndrome and even asthma can all result from being battered. In addition, head injury can lead to the development of epilepsy.

Chronic, intractable pain in many areas of the body is also very common in abused women. The face and the pelvis are two of the more frequent sites in my experience. The pain is not necessarily the result of injury in that particular area, and diagnostic tests are frequently unhelpful, but the pain is all too real.

Always on my mind

In common with all life-threatening traumas, such as war and plane crashes, domestic violence inflicts deep psychological wounds on women who are battered. Such symptoms include:

- loss of self-esteem
- negative views of self
- decreased levels of personal control
- fear
- loss of confidence
- guilt
- feelings of weakness
- increased vulnerability
- anxiety
- poor concentration
- irritability
- anger
- a trapped feeling
- suicidal thoughts.

The track of the emotional roller-coaster which abused women ride defies complete analysis. Many women think that they are going crazy as the switchback hurtles into yet another disorienting loop before twisting them back into the same position they were in before. There are some parts of the ride which almost all women experience, leading to coping responses which, though they are understandable, frequently backfire.

The phantom of fear

In my situation there was a lot of fear. I went to bed afraid and I woke up afraid the whole day long, not knowing what he'd do. If I had a bath, he'd come in with an electric fire plugged in the next room. And he'd just stand there, holding it over me. He never dropped it or said anything. He just liked watching me naked and afraid.

A woman with a partner like this has every reason to be afraid, and taking precautions may literally save her life. Fear has to do with the unknown and incomprehensible. The power of abusive behaviour stems in part from its unpredictability and the fact that the victim cannot make sense of it.

When a woman is assaulted by her intimate partner she wants to understand why the attack has happened. The need for explanation runs very deep in our human psyche. Explanations can certainly help us to cope, but in seeking to explain her husband's behaviour the battered woman runs the danger of excusing him (see p. 32). Some women also make the situation worse by blaming themselves. If a battered woman answers the question 'What made him do it?' with 'I did', she further victimises herself. Since she 'made him do it', she is clearly the one who needs to change. She thus becomes an accomplice to her own battery. If she regards his violence merely as a symptom of his distress, she will tend to ignore her own suffering.

The shroud of shame

Shame is that painful feeling we have when something isn't right. Either we or others whom we care about are out of place, exposed – perhaps even slightly ridiculous. The battered woman feels doubly shamed: she's ashamed both of her husband's behaviour and of her own inability to cope with or stop it.

It was the public aspect of it all that was so humiliating. He'd sometimes whisper to me about some affair as if he was confiding a great secret, when the whole estate knew he was sleeping with lots of other women.

Shame is linked very closely with guilt – the feeling that one is responsible for the shame. The battered woman often feels guilty whatever she does. If she stays with her husband or partner she feels guilty about remaining with a man who continues to assault her; if she leaves, she feels guilty about not having tried hard enough.

The coping mechanisms for guilt and shame often involve minimising ('It's not really so bad; I bet others have to put up with a lot worse') or denial ('He didn't mean to hit me that hard; I'm sure he'll never do it again'). Living with such delusions may help for a while, but either reality will break through eventually, or the intensity of the pain will be alleviated only by the emotional numbing of depression.

The paralysis of powerlessness

We were brought up to debate in our family, but when I dared to question his opinion, I'd get hit even more.

Depression is often associated with powerlessness. Being in a position where, no matter what you do, there is no likelihood of reward is guaranteed to depress, and that's exactly where the battered woman is. Whether or not she seeks to retaliate in some way, she cannot win.

Violence is, by definition, the use of physical force by one person against another to inflict injury or damage. The biological differences between men and women tend to give men an advantage in any violent conflict. The greater muscle bulk and superior physical strength of men overall will always create a disparity of power. Women cannot ignore or overcome this general physical supremacy (although, of course, there will be exceptions!).

If a man chooses not to attack his wife, this is commended as a good moral choice, whereas it is taken for granted that a woman will not attack her husband. Non-aggression for women is therefore a kind of non-power also. The same disparity obviously applies as much to the *threat* of violence as it does to *actual* violence. In this no-win situation, frustration and resentment often boil up into uncontrolled provocation and anger.

> *He said, 'You think I'm stupid. I'm not a boy; I'm a man,' and then he hit me. Something inside me snapped back. 'Does that make you feel more like a man now you've hit me?' Then he broke my jaw.*

Shattered lives

Given the psychological stresss that battered women find themselves under, it is hardly surprising that among them there is a marked incidence of suicide attempts and mental illness. Heavy smoking, alcohol abuse and drug addiction are also more prevalent among battered women than among those who do not experience violence.

In 1984 Leonora Walker, in her book *The Battered Woman Syndrome*,[1] described a clinical syndrome consisting of anxiety, depression and distorted perception, including memory loss, social isolation, disruption of interpersonal relationships and flashbacks of traumatic events. More recent research has also shown a high incidence of:

- Obsessive/compulsive disorders Persistent and intrusive ideas invade the mind and, though they are recognised as senseless or repulsive, they cannot be dismissed. Compulsive behaviour, such as constantly checking the door is locked, results from acting on such thoughts.

27

- Phobias Intense fear in response to a specific stimulus such as spiders or heights or to more generalised situations.
- Panic attacks Overwhelming sensations of acute anxiety, giving multiple symptoms such as sweating, palpitations, tremor, breathlessness, nausea and giddiness.
- Post-traumatic stress disorder The battering is re-experienced in recurrent intrusive recollections by day and dreams at night. Intense distress occurs when a woman is exposed to situations and events which represent elements of the abuse. This leads to persistent avoidance of anything which brings back memories of the trauma, and significant restriction of activity and feelings of detachment from reality can result.
- Sexual difficulties Domestic violence can lead to lack of interest in sex, pain during intercourse, inability to reach orgasm or no pleasure from sex.

The relationship between sex and violence is so important that I will consider it here in greater detail.

Dead sexy

To be close enough to kiss means being near enough to be knifed. Love and hatred, passion and rage, violence and intimacy: all are closely intertwined in our human experience. The view that all violence is related to sexual frustration may be overstating the case – but only just.

An element of danger, and even aggression, can sometimes heighten erotic arousal within strong, loving sexual relationships, but in marriages where respect and tenderness have long gone, the combination of sexual hunger and violent tendencies will often be frightening and may occasionally prove fatal.

> *In my marriage I just had to put up with sex, and as often as I could, I got out of it. It was always 'Get your knickers off; I'm coming to get you.' I remember the sheer terror of that.*

The pain of being hit across the face is not likely to increase an abused wife's feelings of warmth and sexual responsiveness towards her husband. As the capacity for tender and loving sex diminishes, so the likelihood of forced and violent sex increases.

Intercourse against a woman's will and without her consent is very common in violent marriages and partnerships. The disclosure of unwanted sexual experiences in marriage is more difficult for many women than revelation of other types of sexual abuse, such as incest or rape by a stranger. Nevertheless, studies of battered women show that between a third and half have suffered marital rape, usually repeatedly.[2]

This type of sexual abuse is far removed from the sanitised stereotype of the bedroom quarrel. Woman may be hit, kicked or even burned during intercourse. They may have objects such as candlesticks or knives thrust into their vagina or anus. One victim was regularly choked by her husband during sex until she became unconscious. Men who both batter and rape are, in fact, likely eventually to kill their partner. They are also more likely to assault their wives during pregnancy.

Around 10–20 per cent of pregnant women report at least one episode of physical violence during pregnancy, and a quarter of women in one survey said that they had been hit during the six weeks after delivery.[3]

During pregnancy, attacks to the breasts, genitals and abdomen are reported to be more common, and as we saw earlier (p. 7) miscarriage, premature labour or stillbirth can result. There is also a noticeable incidence of low-birth-weight babies among battered mothers. Whether or not violent attacks from abusive partners are more common overall during pregnancy is a matter of considerable debate. What is clear, however, is that in abusive relationships pregnancy certainly makes a woman no less vulnerable to violence.

When such murderous fury is directed simultaneously at a wife who can only partly defend herself and her unborn child who is totally defenceless, many people would ask the question that so often surfaces in connection with domestic violence: 'Why doesn't she leave him?' We'll look at this issue in the next chapter.

4

Coming Back for More

Why Battered Women Stay

'Beat me, beat me. Beat me, beat me. I'll endure your every blow.'

Zerlina in Mozart's *Don Giovanni*

I'll never forget my first encounter with a battered woman. Anita had come to see me about a persistent cough, but when I examined her it was obvious from the multiple bruises on her torso and limbs that the cough wasn't her only problem.

'How did you get these?' I asked.

'Boyfriend,' she murmured.

'First time?'

'Oh, no!'

I was a young and inexperienced GP then and simply couldn't understand why she hadn't left him long ago. A decade later I think I understand a little better.

Love is blind

A major reason for a woman staying with her abusive husband or partner is the same one that initially attracts her to him – she loves him. Many wife-batterers have a charming and winsome side to their personalities that seems to outweigh potential problems, even when the latter can be foreseen.

Everybody liked him. He was quite demanding even then, but this was all part of the attraction.

Funny? He was so comical. I even liked his jealousy to begin with. It was nice, but it the end I felt trapped by it.

A woman in an abusive marriage or partnership has seen the best side of her man as well as his worst. She never loves the violence, but she does love the good things she remembers in him and will often do all she can to excuse him. She just wants the violence to stop.

I don't believe the 'Mr Hyde' that Mike becomes is really him – I married a kind, gentle person. He says he wants to stop doing this, and I believe him – he's started going to a counsellor. Maybe a braver woman would walk away, but I don't want our marriage to end; it's only just begun. We love each other and share the same interests.

It's lovely when it stops

Violence in marriage never occurs without a break. Leonora Walker describes a 'cycle of violence' consisting of three phases:[1]

- Tension building Relatively minor episodes of abuse occur which the wife learns to avoid by keeping out of his way. She does not allow herself to show her anger towards her husband, and may even blame herself.
- Acute battering The husband loses all control, and violence escalates to a climax. The wife may become overtly angry during this phase and be battered even more severely as a result.
- Contrition The abuser belatedly recognises that he has gone too far and makes some effort to patch things up. He

becomes kind and placid for a while and seeks forgiveness from his wife. When her love and affection is given, a **traumatic bonding** occurs with him. She convinces herself that all will now be well. This transient fantasy soon evaporates, however, as the cycle of abuse starts all over again. As the violence continues, it tends to accelerate, with less and less likelihood of even a semblance of regret by the husband.

After he'd punched me, he was remorseful and promised it wouldn't happen again. It didn't for two months, then it became more frequent. Now it's every two weeks.

Puppet on a string

Batterers are often master manipulators and know just how far they can go before pulling back. They also have an uncanny knack of making it seem as if they are the innocent one and their partner is to blame.

Often I was too scared to sleep because that was when he'd usually hit me. Then every morning he'd tell me I'd imagined the whole thing and it hadn't really happened at all.

He seemed to believe in equality, like me; he'd even do the cooking and cleaning. I thought, it's got to be me. But then I began to realise that it was all part of the game, a carefully crafted mask to make others think, 'What a wonderful man she's married,' when all the time he was systematically belittling me every bit as much as when he was actually hitting me.

Nobody understands out there

There is still more than a remnant in society at large that considers unwashed dishes, a meal not ready on time or the refusal of 'conjugal rights' as justifiable provocations of violence. It usually takes a great deal of courage for a battered woman to turn for help, and if she encounters hostility, is disbelieved or trivialised at the first door she tries, she may not try another.

> *The police were not very helpful at that time. He'd smashed up nearly everything I'd got, because he knew that would hurt, and the policeman, when he arrived, grinned at him and said, 'Didn't she cook your dinner, then?'*

Perhaps instead of 'Why does she stay?' a more fruitful question might be 'What is it about our community that is keeping her there?'

She loves it really

Much of the victim-blaming that goes on, even among professionals who should know better, stems from the idea of Freud that masochism – the striving for sexual satisfaction through pain and suffering – is the 'essential nature of women'.[2] More recent descriptions of battered women, using such stereotypical labels as 'Fanny the Flirt' and 'Go-go Gloria',[3] further illustrate the tendency of psychiatry to cast the woman in the role of villain. Blaming the victim in this way may be a defence mechanism that permits professionals to feel less vulnerable and allows them to avoid asking difficult questions about themselves such as 'Isn't it really my responsibility to help?' At the same time the possibility of contamination by the victim can be avoided. If the battered wife is to blame, why should anyone go out of their way to help her? It is the fear of just such a response from others that may sentence the woman to a longer term of silent suffering and encourage her to stay.

Too weak to resist

Sometimes the reasons why a woman stays with her abuser are not so subtle as the above. She may be too shattered to consider anything else. In the initial phase of battery (known as the **impact phase**), women experience shock, numbness and disbelief. This is followed by a state known as **traumatic infantilism**, where she regresses to using the coping mechanisms of childhood and becomes wholly compliant to the aggressor's will. Finally depression sets in and renders her further incapable of breaking out.

The web of fear

A complex network of fears frequently prevents women from leaving abusive relationships. They may fear what might happen to them or their children if they leave.

I had a real fear of going. He said, 'I'll find you wherever you go,' and he meant it. He sent hit-men up to Coventry to watch my mother's house in case I went there.

When I came to the Women's Aid centre, I was even afraid to talk about it because I was told for fourteen years, 'You don't say nothing to nobody.' He threatened the girls too: 'If you tell anybody that Daddy beats Mama, Daddy's gonna get you.' And I was scared to talk, and the girls too.

Understandably other fears arise about the future. Where will she go if she leaves, and how will she survive? Normally if we intend to go off on a short holiday, even just for a few days, we will go down to the travel agent and spend time looking through a variety of brochures for accommodation not only that we can afford but also that we consider suitable for us and our children in terms of safety and comfort. Yet we often expect the battered woman to uproot herself at a moment's notice, not knowing anything about where she might end up, or how long she may have to stay there, let alone what will happen to her children. The fear of having their children taken away from them and put into care is a very real one for many battered mothers.

Financial worries are another potent source of fear. The financial costs of leaving home can be very high. The average income for a two-parent family is nearly two and a half times the average for a single-parent family. This fact can deter some women from leaving, though others may already be poor as a result of their husbands' drinking or gambling, and for them the decision to leave may be easier.

Waiting for God

Religious beliefs will not protect a woman from assault, but in discouraging marital dissolution they can increase her susceptibility to being victimised. While some battered women find that their faith helps them to cope with their suffering and gives them strength and comfort, others lose their faith altogether, especially if the batterer claims religious justification for his behaviour.

For many Christian women, there is tremendous pressure from their church culture to stay with their husbands, come what may. Bland assurances of God's protection are easy to dispense from the safety of the pulpit, and a patriarchal interpretation is often imposed on biblical texts that are used to dissuade women from leaving the marital home to escape violence. Let us look at the two most frequently cited examples in greater detail.

'Wives submit to your husbands as to the Lord. For the husband is the head of the wife as Christ is the head of the church'

(Ephesians 5:22–3). The word 'submit' here means 'accommodate' or 'give way to'. There is no justification for turning submission into a one-way street. The previous verse reads, 'Submit to one another out of reverence for Christ,' and verse 25 commands husbands to love their wives in the same way that Christ loved the Church and died for her sake. The batterer, however, reverses this injunction and risks his wife's life for his own sake.

The concept of the husband being 'the head of the wife' is often used to assert his authority, but the Greek word for head, *kephale*, can mean 'source' or 'beginning' as well as 'authority' or 'boss'. The intended image is therefore likely to be that of a husband nurturing or replenishing his wife rather than ordering her about. Another passage, Colossians 3:19, spells this out even more clearly: 'Husbands, love your wives and do not be harsh with them.'

'Therefore what God has joined together, let man not separate' (Matthew 19:6). Divorce is certainly strongly discouraged in the Bible. To prove the point, these words of Jesus are often coupled with the statement in Malachi, '"I hate divorce," says the Lord God of Israel.' But not many of those who quote this know that it continues, '"and I hate a man's covering himself [or his wife] with violence as well as with his garment," says the Lord Almighty.'[4] The man who resorts to violence with as much ease as putting on his shirt meets with exactly the same censure as divorce. The woman facing the daily reality of violence and the future possibility of divorce has to choose between two evils, not just one. There are no easy answers for her.

A persistently violent husband will usually kill his wife and will have killed the marriage long before that. It is the violence that separates what God has joined together, not the wife who runs for her life to escape from it. Much as the Church may like to look the other way, there are, sadly, situations where divorce is often the only option apart from the mortuary slab.

Christianity is not, of course, the only faith that may present very painful dilemmas for abused women. Other religions, such as Judaism and Islam, also have strong patriarchal traditions that can be misused to force women into remaining in abusive situations indefinitely. For such women, leaving their spouse can seem not only a failure in personal terms but also a betrayal of the tenets and norms of their community. It can require great courage to end a marriage in such circumstances. Women who are forced to do so deserve support and help rather than condemnation.

He's having counselling

Every woman with an abusive partner, even one who is contemplating leaving him, hopes that he will change. There are several counselling programmes available for abusive men, and when a batterer enrols in one this understandably gives his wife renewed hope.

Some men do indeed change and undergo remarkable transformations in their lifestyles. (This is discussed further in chapter 8.) Other men embark on counselling not because they have any desire to change but because they are compelled to as part of a probation order or because they think it will help to persuade their partners to take them back.

It also needs to be borne in mind that, although the battering may stop, verbal and emotional abuse, which is much more difficult to control, may continue, and other associated problems may remain untouched by programmes that target control of violence.

After John started counselling he never hit me again, but his gambling continued just as before. He'd draw his dole money, and before he'd even come home with it he'd blown the lot on the machines. I was having to support him all the time, and I couldn't see it changing, so in the end I asked him to leave.

For the children's sake

The growing evidence that divorce is bad for children[5] has been given wide publicity in recent years, and their children's welfare is a major factor that encourages women to remain in abusive marriages. As a general rule, children do prefer their parents to stay together, rather than divorce, no matter how conflictual the relationship.

In situations of severe battery, however, there is no universal best option. In over half the cases where wife-battering occurs, the children are also at risk of abuse, and the detrimental effects of domestic violence on children can be seen in many ways, some of which are considered in the next chapter.

5

Not in Front of the Children

The Hidden Victims

Be careful what you say, children will listen.
Careful the things you do, children will see.

Stephen Sondheim, *Into the Woods*

Children learn what they live, as the witch in Sondheim's musical makes clear. Children who witness their mother being battered are no exception in learning from the experience. The capacity of children to pick such things up and incorporate them in their own behaviour is often underestimated by parents: combined with the tendency of battered women to minimise the extent of their abuse, its effect on their children may go unnoticed.

He never started on me until after Abigail was in bed. I thought she didn't know until one morning – she must have been about five or six at the time – she looked up at me and asked, 'Did Daddy hurt you again?'

People think children are stupid, like dumb animals ... They say, 'They're only young, it doesn't matter,' but I'd say kids know exactly what is going on.

How do children know? In a recent survey by the charity NCH Action for Children, nearly three-quarters of the chil-

40

dren from violent homes had witnessed attacks on their mother. Two-thirds of them had overheard other episodes of violence.[1]

> *They would yell really loud and scream and when I woke up I heard . . . banging and screaming: it made me scared. Sometimes Mum got scared and she would sit in the corner of our room while we were still in our beds, and he'd come in and shout, 'Get out of here and come and fight like a real woman,' and I'd say, 'Mum doesn't like fighting with you, and I don't like you guys fighting at all.'*
>
> *Eight-year-old*

Nearly all the children surveyed (99 per cent) had seen their mothers crying or distressed at some point, and half had seen their mothers' injuries. Over two-thirds were aware of the atmosphere at home being frightening and not right somehow.

He just had an aura around him, like it made you frightened all the time.

Less than a fifth of mothers had actually discussed the violence with their children. This sometimes added to a child's sense of isolation.

> *I sort of felt pushed out, until she really sat down and told me and then I sort of understood.*

The hidden victims

If it seems incredible that spouse-abuse did not become a matter of general public awareness until the 1970s, it seems even more incredible that only in the 1990s has research and media interest begun to focus on the effects of domestic violence on children. Children whose mothers are battered may be harmed in a variety of ways.

They are exposed to violent or violence-tolerating role models
Sons who witness their father's violence have a ten times greater chance of later perpetrating abuse themselves than those from non-violent families.[2] A large majority of women who are victims of domestic violence come from homes where they witnessed violence.

They are exposed to the marital conflict which accompanies the violence
Even in the absence of violence, children from families with high levels of conflict show a two- to threefold increase in a wide range of symptoms of ill-health.

They may become the victims of abuse themselves
This may happen incidentally – for example, when a brick hurled at the mother hits the child in the face instead. However, we have already seen (p. 16) that in a third of families in which wife-battery occurs, deliberate physical or sexual abuse of children will also take place. Stepfamilies are particularly at risk. (p. 17)

They are exposed to other problems associated with domestic violence
Children of violent parents stand a much greater chance of witnessing their parents drinking too much or abusing drugs. They may have to move from one home to another frequently too.

They suffer from a wide range of behavioural and psychological problems
These are listed in the table on p. 43, and I will now consider some of them in greater detail.

The Effects on Children of Witnessing Parental Violence

Babies and infants	*Toddlers*	*Older children*	*Teenagers*
Excessive crying	Shyness	Poor motivation	Reluctance to bring friends home
Poor sleep	Poor self-esteem	Nightmares	Anger
Lethargy	Dislike of being touched or held	Eating disorders	Drug-taking
Failure to thrive	Frequent symptoms of illness	Stuttering	Alcohol abuse
	Slow speech development	Nervous tics	Early sexual début
	Aggression: biting and hitting	Depression	Increased suicide risk
	Separation difficulty	Attention-seeking behaviour	Truanting
	Screaming, clinging, tantrums, running off to hide	Drug-taking	Running away from home
		Alcohol abuse	Violent behaviour
		Bed-wetting	
		Lying	
		Stealing	
		Psychosomatic complaints: headaches, stomach-aches	

Short-term damage

Emotional

The most commonly reported reaction of children who witness violence at home is fear. They often have difficulty in sleeping at night and may wake up screaming and crying. By day these children tend to be exceptionally clingy and don't like letting go of their mothers. They may become very quiet, nervous and withdrawn.

> *I'm going to tell everybody to be careful. It's very dangerous if you see your Daddy be mean to your Mummy. You know why it's dangerous? Cause what if Daddy took a knife and they fighted with a knife? And if Mummy took a knife, she would cut Daddy.*
>
> *Four-year-old*

Children feel very confused by the conflicting emotions they experience as a result of witnessing violence. They are embarrassed or ashamed, particularly if their father is violent in front of their friends. They struggle with the ambivalence they often sense towards him – loving him, yet hating what he does. They may become very angry about the situation.

Guilt is another common problem, either because children feel that the violence is somehow their fault or because of the way they react to it. They often think they should be able to stop the battering and are overcome with a sense of powerlessness and hopelessness when they realise they can't. No wonder some become suicidal.

> *You come close to breaking-point. I felt like killing myself a lot of the time, though I never actually did it, thank God, now looking back.*
>
> *Sixteen-year-old*

Coping strategies

● Withdrawal   Children retreat to their room or somewhere they can be on their own. Younger children often find comfort in hugging and talking to soft toys. They may devise an intricate fantasy world into which they can escape.

> *I sit down and talk to my stuffed animals and I imagine that my teddy is real.*
>
> *Eight-year-old*

Sometimes the escape route will not be an imaginary one, and the child will run away from home altogether.

● Protectiveness   Children may feel very anxious about the safety of both their mother and their brothers or sisters and cuddle or cling to them excessively. They may fantasise about attacking their mother's violent partner.

> *Beth was constantly drawing pictures of a man with an axe in his hand and a knife in his stomach.*

● Confrontation   Even very young infants on occasion bravely intervene and confront their mother's abuser, and may protect her simply through their refusal to leave her.

> *One particularly bad time my son came in and intervened . . . He stood right beside me, and my husband had his hand up to hit me again, and my son just looked at him . . . whatever it was, he stopped. I swear he would have killed me that day if it hadn't been for my son.*

The violence witnessed by children may lead to confrontation of another kind. Children are quick to spot how they can use their parents' weaknesses, and they may try to gain advantage over their mothers by turning on them.

If you smack me, I'll tell dad and he'll come and beat you up.

Behavioural

There are two main types of behavioural problem.

Regressive behaviour is when a child seems to drop back a stage in his or her development. Bed-wetting may recur when previously the child had been dry; thumb-sucking may start again. Poor speech development and failure to progress at school are further potential effects of violence on child witnesses.

Aggressive traits are the other main difficulty. Some children soon learn that violence is an effective means of gaining control. They may direct their aggression at siblings, at other children at school or at the abused mother herself in some cases.

I rebelled against her because I didn't understand why she put us through it for all those years. I know she was going through it, but so were we. So I just didn't understand . . . it would be on my mind a lot.

Long-term damage

Some children become violent, aggressive and more difficult to control in the long term. The children themselves regard violence as a normal way of life.

Everyone fights.   *Five-year-old*

If you were in the same room as him, he'd run up to you and punch you, and then he would laugh because he thought it was right.

46

The guilt initially experienced by many children often hardens into anger, bitterness and blame as time progresses. The lack of respect for their mother as well as their father may erupt in violent attacks.

> *My eldest has smashed the house up a couple of times. He goes for the personal things that he knows mean something to me. He does it to his brother's things too. Both those boys are full of anger and hate.*

With other children, the guilt and anger is turned inwards, and they become sad and depressed.

> *I made something big, and it's broke because my Dad's gone and I miss him so much.*
>> *Five-year-old commenting on her drawing of a heart split in half.*

Gender-identity may also be distorted.

> *What the violence did take away from me was my femininity. I was always a dainty little girl until I was about six, but then I started having to be hard all the time. If I was this dainty little girl, I'd have no chance, would I?*

Self-confidence and self-esteem shrivel up and children of abusing partners have difficulty in establishing friendships with others at school. Their education may suffer in several other ways. They may be so distressed and distracted that their concentration is impaired. Protectiveness towards their mother or siblings may mean that they make excuses for not wanting to go to school at all or rush home from school without completing their work 'to make sure Mum's OK'. They may not attend school because they are too shocked or upset to do so after an episode of violence at home. Once they start falling behind in their work, they may never be able to catch up. They then decide that school has nothing to offer them anyway, and so they give up.

They may give up on home too with less than adequate preparation. The average age for leaving home in Britain is twenty-three. Youthful witnesses to violence understandably often leave (or are thrown out) well before that and usually have insufficient emotional and financial resources to cope without turning to crime, drugs or prostitution in order to survive.

When Daddy kills Mummy

If witnessing violence at home can produce so many problems, witnessing parental murder must be the ultimate horror. Around 40 per cent of all female murder victims in the UK are killed by a current or former partner or husband.[3] On average seventy women a year are killed by their partners.

The number of child witnesses is difficult to gauge with any certainty, but a clinic at the Royal Free Hospital in London sees around fifty new cases every year.[4] In the USA, even in the early 1980s, Los Angeles County Sheriff's Homicide Division alone estimated that about 200 children a year witnessed the murder of one parent by the other.[5]

These children face unspeakable disadvantages:

- the simultaneous loss of both parents, one by death and the other by imprisonment or hospitalisation
- dislocation from their home environment and uncertainty about where and with whom they will live
- the stigma of everyone knowing about the murder
- conflicts of loyalty about their parents.

Their needs are immense and are often neglected by professionals such as the police and social services departments who have to cope with the aftermath of murder.

A glimmer in the darkness

The litany of disasters outlined in this chapter needs to be considered by every mother (and anyone who counsels her) who thinks she should automatically stay with her husband or partner because it would be better for the children than divorce. There are no easy options, but there is hope.

Anecdotal evidence certainly shows that not all children are severely affected by witnessing domestic violence, and a few seem hardly damaged at all. Some children enlist the help of friends and relatives in their struggle to survive, and those whose mothers manage to maintain a warm relationship with them in spite of the home circumstances seem to do best.

An important consideration, when a woman is deciding whether to stay or leave for the children's sake, is how the violence is affecting her ability to function as a mother. If she is becoming too depressed and drained of motivation to meet her children's physical and emotional needs or begins to take her own anger and frustration out on them, then it may be the lesser of two evils to leave and try to build a new future away from the violence.

Whether she leaves or stays, a strategy for her own welfare as well as that of her children needs to be planned. Survival tactics are the subject of the next chapter.

6

Survival Tactics

Dealing with Your Violent Partner

Rescue me, O Lord, from evil men;
protect me from men of violence . . .

Psalm 140

This chapter addresses specifically the victims of domestic violence, though I hope it will also be helpful to those who counsel and assist them.

Most women who are beaten by their partners don't want to leave home for a variety of reasons, considered in chapter 4. If you decide to stay, there is much that you can and should do to help and protect yourself and your children.

Breaking the silence

The majority of battered wives say nothing after the first episode. Half will keep the violence a secret even after a year of being assaulted has gone by. Fear, of course, is what holds you back.

What if they don't believe me?

They might think I'm stupid.

If he finds out I've told someone, he'll kill me.

Suppose I tell the wrong person?

My children might be taken away from me.

Some of these fears are groundless. For example, if it is clear that *you* are not responsible for any abuse and have done everything possible to protect your children from it, no one will think of removing them from your care.

Other fears are justified. If you select the wrong person to confide in, an unhelpful or hostile response could set you back considerably. Most women in your position, however, have found that in order for things to change for the better they have had to share the secret eventually – and though it may come as total surprise to some of your friends, others will be relieved to know. When Julia, whose story opens this book, finally told a friend after fifteen years of beatings, her friend said:

I thought there was something funny about you and Tim. You were the strangest couple because you were always so polite to each other. There was never any teasing between you. I suppose if you had said anything remotely teasing, you knew you'd be dealt with.

The right person to tell is someone who will give you time, will listen without passing judgment on you, will treat your disclosure as absolutely confidential and will offer you ongoing support. You will know when you have found such a person because, although it won't be easy to spill the beans, once you've done so you'll feel relieved of a burden. You should be able to hope again and begin to find the strength that you thought had gone for good.

Building your support network

Part of your partner's strategy of breaking your spirit down will have been to isolate you from friends and family. Now that you have had the courage to tell someone about your true situation, you should seek to build and expand your support network once again.

Family members who you think will understand should be told when you feel able to do so. It is also worth contacting the increasing number of local and national telephone help-lines for battered women. These are listed at the back of this book.

If there is a support group for women in your situation which meets locally, this can be a tremendous help, both in reassuring you that you are not alone and in providing further contacts for practical assistance.

You may also want to seek the help of a counsellor to work through some of the emotional conflicts and scars left by the abuse you have endured. Take care in your choice. At the present time almost anyone in Britain can call themselves a counsellor, though this unsatisfactory situation is gradually being tightened up. Some accredited counselling agencies are listed in the appendix.

Involving the police

If you remain at home with a violent partner, you should call the police if you are attacked. Domestic violence is a crime, and to suffer it in silence is to do yourself an injustice. Calling the police in itself may serve to protect you from further assault, even if they take no further action.

In one study 41 per cent of married women who were attacked by their husbands or ex-husbands but did not call the police were assaulted again within an average of six months, compared with a repeat-assault incidence of only 15 per cent for wives who had called the police.[1]

In the past the police had a reputation for not wanting to get involved with cases of domestic violence. This is rapidly changing, however, and as a result of their increasing awareness of, and training in, domestic-violence issues you should always be treated by the police with professionalism and understanding. Most police forces now have dedicated domestic-violence units or vulnerable persons units with specially trained police, including women officers, who will give you the opportunity to talk about your difficulties away from your partner.

All the options open to you will be explained in simple terms, and contacting the police in no way commits you to court proceedings. Where no criminal proceedings are to follow the police can still:

- advise you about Women's Aid centres, victim-support groups and other helpful organisations; they can also advise about instigating civil proceedings
- facilitate the treatment and recording of any injuries you sustain and encourage the reporting of further incidents to them
- provide protection and escort you home should you wish to collect any personal belongings.

When criminal proceedings are to follow, you should be prepared to attend court and give evidence. In these circumstances the police will, if required, arrest your partner, interview him and charge him with the appropriate criminal offence if there is sufficient evidence to do so. The most common offences are the following.

- Common assault   This covers less serious violence such as pushing, threats, and slaps without any resulting injury.

- Assault occasioning actual bodily harm   This, as its name suggests, entails actual injury such as bruising and cuts.
- Malicious wounding or inflicting grievous bodily harm   This involves an assault with or without a weapon from which the injuries are very serious.
- Malicious wounding or inflicting grievous bodily harm with intent to do so   As above but this includes the deliberate intent to inflict the injury. This is a very serious offence, which is reflected in the fact that it carries life imprisonment as a possible penalty.

With the exception of common assault, all of the above are arrestable offences, and in certain circumstances power of arrest for common assault is possible, though most cases can be pursued only by means of a private prosecution.

If your husband or partner has been charged with a criminal offence, the matter will be taken over by the Crown Prosecution Service (CPS). At this stage it is not unusual for you to come under pressure from your husband and his friends and relatives to drop proceedings, or you may yourself decide to do so. In these circumstances the police will talk to you and convey your wishes to the CPS, which will usually follow your request. Only in very exceptional cases, when the CPS decides it is in your or the public interest to proceed with the case, would it discuss the situation fully with you and then apply to the court for a witness summons to ensure that you attend court.

The police will also:

- obtain evidence, including medical evidence from casualty departments or from your GP, including, where appropriate, photographic evidence of injuries
- ensure that your husband or partner appears in court at the earliest opportunity; the court will usually impose conditions of non-contact on his bail conditions

- inform you of progress at each stage of the proceedings and normally accompany you to court.

Making use of the law

In 1976 measures were introduced in civil law whereby women could seek some protection for themselves from domestic violence. The Domestic Violence and Matrimonial Proceedings Act made it possible for you to seek an injunction. (At the time of writing, the Government is proposing new measures to strengthen this protection.)

Injunctions

An injunction is simply an order from a county court telling a person to do or not to do something. In domestic-violence cases the injunction is usually intended to prevent your partner from attacking you and/or entering the home.

A **non-molestation injunction** orders your partner not to assault, harass or interfere with you, or to attempt to do so, or to encourage any other person to do so. An **ouster injunction** can order your partner to vacate your home, forbid your partner entry to the home or to approach within a specified number of yards of it. It can also order your own access to the home.

The majority of injunctions are heard *inter-partes*, which means that your partner is given notice of the court hearing and has a chance to put his case. Such an injunction usually takes between three and five weeks to get to court and, if granted, usually has a time limit of three months, although this limit can be extended.

Your partner's solicitor may suggest to the judge that your partner gives an **undertaking** to the court instead of your having an injunction granted. An undertaking is a promise he makes to the court, which has the advantage that you do not have to appear to give evidence in person, but if he breaks his undertaking, *you* and not the police have to apply to the court to have him penalised.

An injunction offers the advantage that it can have a **power of arrest** attached to it. This offers you a much greater degree of protection but can be requested only if you are either married or living as man and wife. Evidence of recent actual bodily harm (see p. 54) must usually be produced if you are requesting power of arrest.

When granted, power of arrest means that the police can arrest your husband immediately they have reason to believe him to be in breach of the injunction. He must then be brought within twenty-four hours before a judge, who has discretion to commit him to prison for a period ranging from three weeks to six months. Although in theory this ought to confer considerable protection on you, unfortunately I often hear of cases in which injunctions are flouted and judges do nothing about it.

When no power of arrest is given, if your injunction is breached you yourself must make an application to the court to commit your partner or husband to prison. This can be a very lengthy procedure.

An *inter-partes* injunction is of no use if you are in grave and immediate danger. You should seek police protection or a place of refuge while applying to the county court for a *ex-parte* injunction, which can be granted within twenty-four hours. *Ex-parte* means that your partner does not have to attend court in order for the injunction to be granted. Such injunctions are granted, however, only in the most extreme circumstances and usually remain in force for just a few days while your partner is served with the order and requested to attend court for another hearing later.

One practical difficulty, even with an *ex-parte* injunction, is that it is effective only after it is served on your partner in person. If he is elusive or his whereabouts are not known, this makes personal serving impossible, but powers of arrest can be made effective prior to personal service of the injunction on your partner.

Protection orders
These are similar to injunctions but are given by a magistrates' court and are available only if you are married.

Although you can apply to the courts directly, you will probably engage a solicitor. The police, Women's Aid or the Solicitor's Family Law Association will advise you of solicitors with special expertise in domestic-violence cases. You may be able to qualify for legal aid, your eligibility being assessed on your income, the number of your dependent children and your savings. If you are on social-security benefits, you should automatically qualify for legal aid, which can be granted quickly on an emergency basis, if necessary.

If your partner has been prosecuted and you have suffered bodily harm (see p. 52), it is possible to apply for compensation to the Criminal Injuries Compensation Board, whose address is listed at the end of the book. (p. 100).

Ground rules

Whether or not you decide to obtain protection under the law, you should draw up ground rules about what is acceptable and unacceptable if you are to continue to live with your husband or partner, and you must make these quite clear to him.

The rules will vary from couple to couple, but the following are often useful.

● The 'time-out' rule. If you feel threatened in any way, whether or not he agrees with your assessment, you will say firmly 'time out,' and he must leave the room (or the house) straight away.

- There is to be no more abuse, and that includes withholding money, swearing and cursing at you, and putting you down as well as hitting you.
- He will not stop you from going out to work if you choose or seeing your family and friends when you want.
- He is not to hit the children or intimidate them.

Once the rules have been agreed, stick to them.

Plan for emergencies

If, in spite of your best efforts, things do not change for the better or deteriorate, you should have a contingency plan for emergencies. You should do the following things.

- Keep secure a file containing all important documents you may need, including birth certificate(s), marriage certificate, bank and building society books, insurance policies, cheque book, credit cards, rent book and receipts, child-allowance book, passport, address and phone book, driving licence, copies of any injunctions or court orders, repeat prescriptions and medical cards, and a recent photograph of your spouse or partner in case the police need to trace him.
- Memorise, or always have with you, the number of the local Women's Aid helpline or refuge.
- Get an extra set of house and car keys cut, and keep them safe.
- Have a small bag ready packed with clothing and essentials for you and your children.
- If you have told the children (see p. 61–2), do practise

emergency escape drills with them. Help them to practise calling the police or the local Women's Aid helpline.

- If you have told a neighbour or nearby friend about your situation, devise some kind of emergency signal that they will recognise if you need them to summon help urgently.

Remember that these provisions need not undermine your determination to make things work as far as you are concerned. They may, however, save your life and your children's if things turn critical.

The final straw

If things don't work out, leaving your partner for good is still likely to be one of the most difficult decisions you will ever make. Writing down a list of the pros and cons of leaving may be helpful, but in practice most women find that a change of circumstances suddenly provides the final impetus to go. Such events commonly include:

- a narrow escape from death or a particularly savage attack

The last time he put me in hospital for three months. I knew that one more beating would kill me, and I had a choice to make. I either left and made a new start or I died. It was that simple.

- physical attacks taking on a different pattern

I tried to bide my time until the children were ready to go to college. Then one day I turned up unexpectedly to pick him up from work, and in front of everybody he grabbed me by the hair and pulled me into the fire escape and hit me really hard across the face. Until then his abuse had been contained in the house –

now other people knew about it, and for some reason it made me wake up. I left a few days later with the children.

● abuse involving new areas

   When he said I must make a complete and utter break from my family, I realised then that he held no more appeal for me whatsoever. It was hard enough for me to have access to my friends. Soon there would be nothing for me anyway, so I left.

● someone alters your perspective

   My sister came to stay with me for a few days, and memories of how I used to be came flooding back. I suddenly realised that life hadn't always been this present hell and that it didn't have to be hell any longer. I made up my mind then to leave him.

● violence directly affecting children for the first time.

   The final straw was an argument over £10 for a pizza. He threw a metal bin at me while my son was trying to separate us. My son had never intervened before, but I heard him say, 'Daddy, don't hit Mummy.' I didn't want my son to think that this was normal life, so I left.

Taking leave of him

Leaving will be hard. There is no way of making it painless, but the knowledge that you have tried every other possible option will help to ease the pain, as will giving adequate thought and preparation to your departure.

Why shouldn't he go?

You may understandably feel angry that you are the one who has to run away when your partner is the guilty party. Why shouldn't he have to look for a new home? After all, the stress of a broken marriage is hard enough for you to bear without the hassle of having to find accommodation for you and your children.

The difficulty is often that the law cannot usually provide the total protection you may feel you need. You can, as we have seen, apply to the county or magistrates' court for an ouster injunction or an exclusion order, but this takes time and money, and at the end of the day you may still not feel safe knowing that your partner is aware of exactly where to find you.

> *I just felt like a sitting duck waiting for the attack to happen. I couldn't stand the strain of it, so I left in the end.*

If you do stay in your home after your husband has been removed, you should, of course, ensure that all the locks and your telephone number are changed.

Should I tell the children?

Whether you share with your children in advance about your decision will depend on their age and level of understanding.

Very young children, even if told in simple terms that they can grasp, may accidentally spill the beans to your husband about the 'little trip' they are going on with you. This could endanger your life. The knowledge that a woman is leaving frequently precipitates her murder.

If you tell older children, do so simply, without too much detail. Make your plans sound as positive as you honestly can. Don't criticise their father (they still have to relate to him

61

even after they have left with you and will form their own opinions from what they have seen and heard). It is a good idea to let them pack their own bag of favourite clothes and toys, if possible, so that they retain at least some measure of control for themselves in the situation.

Except in the most extreme circumstances you should not leave your children behind with your abusive partner. This may expose them to mortal danger if he decides to exact revenge on them, and you may find it difficult to get the children back again later.

Where will I go?
If you are fortunate enough to have a large disposable income, renting a flat or even moving into a hotel are possibilities, but it is likely that money will be in short supply, as separation is usually a costly business for both partners, even when the complications of violence are not involved.

Family and friends may be another possibility for you. It is likely to impose a considerable strain on them if you arrive without any warning, so it is best to discuss the situation with them first, if possible. The safety factor is an important one to consider.

I went to my parents but I was a nervous wreck. If the phone went I started shaking.

If you have to leave your home because of violence you are legally considered homeless, and the local authority has a statutory duty to provide you with accommodation. In practice, however, this may be difficult to secure.

I went to the council and they said, 'But can you give us any proof?' so I said, 'Yeah, I'll come back dead next week!'

Each year around 45,000 women and children in England alone are accommodated in the refuges run by Women's Aid. Although the refuges were started as far back as 1971 and there are now nearly 300 in Britain, myths about them still abound. If you or your family and friends are concerned that you might end up in some gloomy basement in a condemned house, let me assure you that this will not be the case.

The refuges for which I provide medical cover are indistinguishable from the other houses in the street and, in some cases, are some of the smartest ones in an already pleasant neighbourhood.

This place is a sanctuary. It's clean, warm, safe – and you can have a decent conversation. I haven't had one of those in years.

If you are thinking of going to a refuge you need to know the following information.

- It's not a derelict building.
- There are no wardens, few rules and no judgments.
- Support and encouragement will be available.
- You'll be helped to obtain benefits and legal advice.
- Local schools will take your children, and transport to and from school is sometimes available.
- Medical cover (including emergencies) and preventative health services will be provided free.
- There is no time limit to your stay.
- You will pay a weekly amount that reflects your ability to pay.

You should be aware that some refuges will only take mothers with children, so it is wise to ring one of the numbers at the back of this book to check your local situation.

What will happen to my children?

If you stay in a refuge it will take time for your children to settle down in a strange environment with new faces all around them. Usually they will quickly make friends among the other children, and it can be very helpful for them to discover that they are not alone in what they are facing.

The majority of refuges have play areas and employ specialist children's workers to supervise activities and to spend time with children if they need a trained listening ear.

Since the 1989 Children's Act came into force in October 1991, courts no longer make over custody or grant access orders. The law now talks in terms of **parental responsibility**. Married parents have joint responsibility and lose it only if the child is subsequently adopted by others. Where parents are unmarried, the mother has sole parental responsibility under the Children's Act. An unmarried father can, however, gain legal parental responsibility either by taking out a Parental Responsibility Agreement or by making an application to the court.

When parents separate (whether married or not), the court can issue any or all of a group of four orders known as **Section 8 Orders**.

- A residence order states with which parent the child will have his or her home.
- A contact order specifies how much contact the child can have with the parent with whom she or he is not living. The emphasis of a contact order is on your children's right to have contact with your partner rather than your partner's right to have access to your children. Specific details can be attached to the order, specifying, for example, places and times where such contact can occur.
- A specific-issue order settles a particular dispute about the child's life, such as which religion they should be brought up in or which school they should attend.

● A prohibited-steps order prevents some specific action being taken with the child – removal to another country, for example.

Section 8 orders can have a power of arrest attached to them, and you should apply for this if there is good evidence that your husband or partner may breach the order.

It is not often possible now for one parent to have total care and control of the children, and the Children's Act forbids the court from making any Section 8 orders unless they are of benefit to the child concerned. You may experience difficulty in getting statutory state benefits for your child without the proof provided by a residence order, for example, and your solicitor should make it clear to the court that your child will benefit if the order is granted.

Reclaiming your life

Leaving your partner need not be the end for you but a new beginning. You can now start to rebuild your life.

Financial stability
Your local Citizen's Advice Bureau or Women's Aid helpline should be able to give you expert advice on what benefits and allowances you can claim. You may also want to find a job. Being in a refuge can be a stigma when making job applications, and some of the women I have talked to felt it had prejudiced their chances at interview. In the long term, however, failing to tell the truth is likely to land you in even greater difficulty. You know from your own experience what lies can lead to.

Emotional healing
You may have suffered years of abuse before making your escape, and the memories and scars of it all are not going to

disappear overnight. It may take several years before you feel truly safe and secure again.

In all probability you will need a lot of support as your emotions roller-coaster from day to day. You may want help with specific problems, such as alcohol addiction. Some useful self-help and support groups are listed at the back of this book. If you are depressed or suffering from severe anxiety, you may benefit from both counselling and anti-depressant therapy. The range of options available is worth discussing with your doctor.

New sexual relationships

It is perfectly normal to be troubled by your sexual feelings when breaking free from an abusive relationship. You may find – particularly if you have been raped by your partner – that you have become very fearful of sexual contact altogether. The possibility of having been exposed to sexually transmitted disease, especially AIDS, can also contribute to sexual anxiety. Your GP, or the sexually transmitted diseases department (often called genito-urinary or G-U medicine departments) of your local hospital, should be able to arrange appropriate counselling and tests.

At the other extreme, you may feel overwhelmed by sexual desire, having been freed at last from your partner's control. Some women in your situation find that they embark upon a string of transient sexual relationships. As I have indicated in my book *Sex and Intimacy*,[2] there is no such thing as casual sex, and eventually it is very likely to exact a high price both from you and from your children.

Divorce or reconciliation

Whatever you decide about divorcing or reconciling yourself with your partner, it has to be what *you* want. Leaving in the first place was difficult because he wasn't all bad. The men who hit the hardest are often the best at making up afterwards. Your having left him may incite your partner to rage, or he may now shower you with presents, promises, attention along with outright lies and deception to try to persuade you to return. You would be wise to wait, for two good reasons.

First, you need to be sure that he really has changed. Many women have returned too soon to their cost and, sometimes, to their death. Even if he enrols in a rehabilitation programme for violent men, there can often be hidden snags (see pp. 84–5), which need to be thought about carefully.

Second, you will be better able to cope with him, and perhaps even begin to love him again, only if you learn to love yourself. Let your friends, your family, the members of your local church or the staff at the refuge take care of you and make you feel you're valued and special and that your life is worth while again. Whether or not you eventually go back to him, you need time to heal as fully as you can.

7

Take It Like a Man

The Battered Husband – Myth or Reality?

There is no excuse for male violence
and too many excuses for female violence.

Erin Pizzey

When I wept in court I was told by my own solicitor to pull myself together because 'the judge won't like that'. They all refused to consider the possibility of a man being victimised by his wife.

Who can blame them? The idea of women beating up their husbands doesn't strike most people as very likely. But then forty years ago the idea of parents abusing their children was equally unthinkable, and it has been only over the past fifteen years that wife-abuse has been generally accepted as a serious problem. As we have seen, it can easily remain hidden; so too can the battering of men by their female intimates.

The invisible men

As I have indicated throughout this book, feminist ideology has provided a great deal of helpful insight into violence against women, but it has little or nothing to contribute to

68

our understanding of female violence against men. Indeed, so predominant is the feminist presence among domestic-violence researchers (understandably so) that there seems to be a determined effort to play female violence down.

Mildred Pagelow of California State University is one leading researcher who in 1992 confidently claimed, 'The battered husband syndrome can be laid to rest, as empirical evidence suggests that the claim was little more than an international headline-grabber in the "man bites dog" tradition.'[1] Yet that same year empirical evidence from a survey of nearly 300 domestic-violence victims presenting to a city hospital casualty department in Britain showed that equal numbers of men and women were assaulted.[2] More surprisingly, the researchers found that men received more serious injuries than women and lost consciousness more often. Even Pagelow eventually concedes in her article that at least 5 per cent of battered spouses are husbands and admits this is a 'serious problem'.[3]

Figures collected by police domestic violence units in the UK show that the number of men injured by their partners has doubled over the past five years and that 12 per cent of domestic violence victims in 1992 were men – nearly 1,400 cases were reported in London and the West Midlands alone.[4]

The reality of male victimisation is confirmed by those few agencies which offer help to such men. At least a hundred men each year contact the Women's Aid helpline in Swindon, and in south-west London Merton Male, a helpline for male victims and also perpetrators of domestic violence, handles up to fifty calls a day, the majority of which are from male victims.[5] The men who use this helpline range from age twenty-one to eighty and come from all walks of life, from the unemployed and upholsterers to diplomats and doctors. Childwatch, a charity that counsels adults who were abused as children, reports that in its experience violence against men has increased by 20 per cent over the past ten years.[6]

The violent physical abuse of men is a real problem made worse by the extent and depth of denial currently surrounding the subject. I had been in general practice for nearly ten years before I recognised my first case. Before then I would have said the whole idea was ridiculous. Now, having spoken to some male victims and read many gruelling written testimonies of others, I am convinced that they are genuine. Over the next decade domestic assaults on men will become an increasingly recognised fact, but the acceptance of unpalatable truths by society is always a slow business, and it will take time.

Meanwhile, most battered husbands are currently 'defeated by the denial of their problem by the law, doctors and people in general', claims Dr Malcolm George of London University, one of the few researchers investigating female violence. He states: 'As a society we are not conditioned to accept men as victims of women's violence. We accept female victims of male abuse because we think women are always less powerful than men.'[7]

Of course, concern about male vicitimisation has to be balanced against the fact that most research indicates that around 95 per cent of victims are female. Women are by far and away the most frequently abused, and the bulk of this book is therefore dedicated primarily to meeting the needs of women as the principal victims. However, there is no cause for complacency regarding violence *by* women, as we shall now see.

'Hell hath no fury . . .'

Freya is petite and softly spoken, not the sort of girl that you would think capable of violence, yet when she saw her husband Simon looking at another woman at a party, she showed a very different face.

I was so furious I punched his lights out. I straddled him on the floor and just kept kicking and slapping him. Then I lunged at his face and dislocated his jaw.

Robert is a surgeon, and his description to me of his wife's first attack on him illustrates many features common to female violence.

Susan was always asking for things from morning till night and wanted something from the chemist one day to make her nails grow less brittle. They hadn't got a large bottle, so she marched out of the shop in a vile temper. When we got home, she poured herself a drink, and the next minute she was hitting me over the head with her shoes. I was caught totally by surprise and realised that blood was trickling out of my ear. Eventually I managed to hold her by the wrists to try to protect myself, but as soon as I let go she attacked me again. She was biting me, scratching me, just hitting out wildly. I eventually escaped and had to flee the house. When I returned a couple of hours later, she had broken a window and smashed up part of the house. She said I had broken her finger and then phoned the police. When they came, it was I who ended up going down to the station for questioning, since she claimed I had attacked her. I had tinnitus for weeks after that first assault. What the neighbours thought I do not know.

Women who attack their partners come from all social classes and are not necessarily large or exceptionally strong. One detective inspector (who is also a woman) comments: 'Women can be very, very violent. The two most violent people I've ever had to deal with were women ... You could liken men and women fighting to cats and dogs. The dogs may be bigger, but if the cat is cornered, it usually wins.'[8]

Women, unlike cats, will nearly always use weapons during an assault. Items such as bottles, lamps, knives and scissors are often employed and, rather surprisingly, so are baseball bats. Attacks frequently originate from the kitchen, with the women emerging with a heavy pan or knife. Perhaps the kitchen, as well as being a ready source of weaponry, is also the place where hatred boils over as easily as the milk?

Attacks tend to be made when the man is least prepared to defend himself, so they often occur from behind, when the victim is sitting down, or asleep, or in front of the children. Injuries inflicted vary from cigarette burns on the back to knife wounds in the chest.

> *She would kick and punch me without any warning, and on several occasions she stabbed me. She would go for my face, neck, genitals – any part of my body that was available. I still have scars from where she tore my flesh with her nails.*

A sexual element features in many assaults, and the genitalia are a frequent focus of attack. In 1994 the wife of a scaffolder appeared in court in Britain for having poured boiling wax over her husband's genitals, causing 13 per cent burns. In 1992 Lorena Bobbitt in America made world headlines when, in a fit of fury, she severed her husband's penis while he was asleep.

Deadlier than the male?

If women use an arsenal of weaponry to batter men physically, when it comes to other forms of abuse they usually require no help. Just as men abuse their partners in a variety of ways

72

(discussed in chapter 1), women utilise the same spectrum of techniques.

Verbal and psychological abuse are often carried out by lying and innuendo to others about the victim as well as by insulting and cursing him directly.

Tom and Marina go out to a party together, and while Tom gets something to eat Marina is chatting with the girls.

'Tom does look as if he's enjoying himself tonight, Marina' (he has to; he knows what he'll have coming to him if he spoils Marina's evening).

'Does he?' replies Marina mysteriously. 'Of course, you don't know what he's really like at home.'

Having aroused everyone's suspicions with her little seed of doubt, she then changes the subject. 'I shouldn't have said that. I'd pay for it at home if he found out I'd said anything. How was your holiday, Maureen?'

Sleep deprivation is another common form of abuse that men are tormented with.

> *When I fell asleep, she would kick me until I woke up. If I moved into the spare room, she'd pour water over the bed. Finally I took to sleeping on a groundsheet in the car.*

Women are also quite capable of sexual abuse. One of the callers on a male helpline told of how his jealous wife would force him to obtain an erection and ejaculate in front of her when he came home in the evening, so that she could assess the volume of semen to 'check' that he had not been having sex elsewhere.

What makes women violent?

There are many theories about why women attack their partners. Alix Kirsta suggests that 'women turn to violence as a means of economic survival or to escape from the pressures, boredom or isolation of a dead-end existence."[9] This may well be true in some cases, but many of the women who attack their partners are professionals who are very successful in their careers and presumably have a good deal of job satisfaction.

Pre-menstrual syndrome and alcohol abuse are also commonly cited as possible causes of female violence, but there is little evidence that they are influential factors in the majority of cases.

It seems that a change in the balance of power in an intimate relationship can trigger violence in women as well as men. A woman who has learned to dominate others in her job may also seek to dominate her spouse or partner at home and use violence as a means to achieve her aim. Some women who are faced with great pressures at work – the same pressures that many men face – may turn to violence as a way of alleviating the stress. Now that many women want to equal men in the power that they wield, it seems that some may also equal men in the abuse of that power.

Psychologists often make a distinction between **expressive violence**, a sudden outburst of unpremeditated violence, which is said to characterise women, and **instrumental violence**, the calculating, systematised violence usually adopted by battering males. Recently there seems to have been a rise in the use of instrumental violence by women.

Many women who batter their partners have experienced abuse themselves, either in childhood or in previous intimate relationships. The fear of masculinity or the hatred of a domineering ex-husband may precipitate a woman's violence in subsequent partnerships. On the other hand, a perceived lack of masculinity in her husband may fuel a wife's anger and hostility.

> *He was gentle, and I couldn't stand him being so soft. I hit him because I wanted him to fight back and prove he was a real man.*

Of course, women who batter may do so in retaliation for violence done to them by their current partner, but female violence is by no means always provoked by the husband or partner. He may well wonder just what has hit him.

No place to run

The man who is physically assaulted by his wife faces exactly the same kind of emotional reaction that most female victims experience. Most men instinctively think, what did I do wrong to trigger it? and the same reframing of perspective discussed in relation to battered wives (p. 25) is needed to focus male victims on the woman's responsibility for her own violent actions.

The male victim, however, faces huge problems in terms of shame and credibility. David goes into work having been given a black eye by his wife the night before. As he enters the staffroom, what is he going to say to his colleagues when they ask him how he got it? Much easier to say nothing, or to claim that he fell against something, than to confess that his wife did it to him.

Abused men find it hard to accept themselves as victims in domestic situations. It is emasculating to have to confess to it. When the truth is revealed disbelief, even ridicule, is the likely response.

> *I went to my GP to talk about Geraldine's behaviour. The visit was a total waste of time. Too many GPs don't listen to men. They think you must have done something provocative and the woman must be in the right.*

She's 5ft 2in, blonde and beautiful. Whoever is going to believe me?

The most affirming thing that can be done for a victim is to believe his story. Few men make up tales of violence. Indeed, most are very reluctant to talk. Some men who contact the Merton Male helpline just cry the first time they call and can say nothing. Most men have suffered physical abuse for periods of between one and twenty years before even attempting to share their plight. They deserve serious consideration and help now, for their numbers will increase in future.

If you are an abused man youself, what can you do to get help? You should ring the Merton Male line or the Domestic Violence Intervention Project, the numbers of which are listed at the end of the book. In some areas the local police domestic violence unit may offer sympathetic help, but this varies from region to region. GPs can vary in their response too. If you feel you cannot talk to your own GP, you can ring your local health authority, which may be able to give you the name of a doctor with an interest in domestic-violence issues.

At the present time the number of battered women in need of help far exceeds that of battered men (and probably always will), and even though the desperate situation of such women has been highlighted for many years, resources are still inadequate to meet their needs. Preventative intervention is essential to tackle the problem of domestic violence and to help both women and men to avoid becoming perpetrators or victims of it.

Various possible preventative strategies will be examined in the next chapter, which rightly returns the focus to abuse of women. In reading it, however, the fact that men are also the victims of domestic violence should not be forgotten.

8

An End to the Raging

Preventing Domestic Violence

I distrust the incommunicable: it is the source of all violence.

Jean-Paul Sartre

The goal of world peace will always remain out of reach in a global society where vast numbers of women experience untold brutality and violence in their own homes from the men who claim to love them.

Yet the extent of the problem must not be allowed to overshadow the importance of even small attempts to overcome it. Effective strategies to control and prevent domestic violence will never be simple to devise and implement. The hydra never has been an easy beast to slaughter, its multiple heads must be defeated one by one.

In health care, prevention is usually considered to fall into three categories. **Primary prevention** is the attempt to prevent a problem before it ever starts. **Secondary prevention** aims at early detection to prevent it from escalating. **Tertiary prevention** attempts to prevent the relapse of an already well-established problem.

Given the natural human tendency to intervene only when things have reached crisis point, most resources within the field of domestic violence have so far inevitably gone into tertiary prevention. The majority of prevention and intervention programmes operate only once violence is an already established part of a woman's life. Let us look at these programmes first.

After the horse has bolted . . .?

The fact that tertiary prevention intervenes at such a late stage in the progression of wife-battering does not undermine its very real value. Its aims, damage limitation and the prevention of recurrence of the violence, are well worth while.

There are three main aspects of tertiary prevention:

- women's refuges and shelters (see p. 63)
- police intervention and legal controls (see p. 52–7)
- psychological help, which is looked at in greater detail below.

You don't need a psychiatrist: it's his fault

> *I hate victims who respect their executioners.*
> Jean-Paul Sartre, *Les Séquestres d'Altona*

Different ideological perceptions of the root causes of violence against women has led to an unfortunate and, in my view, unnecessary controversy over the purpose of psychological intervention for battered wives.

Some organisations that work with abused women rightly stress as a fundamental principle that the problem is the man's violence and abuse, not the woman's psychology. But to dismiss on this basis any need for healing and therapeutic counselling for the woman is, I think, badly mistaken. Because the woman's psychology is not the cause of the problem does not mean her psychology is not *damaged* by the problem. I invariably find that it is and that appropriate counselling, and the use of psychotherapeutic techniques or indeed drugs (particularly anti-depressants), is of enormous value to the majority of battered women under my care.

When handled sensitively, such an approach need not undermine the self-esteem and integrity of the woman concerned but supplements rather than negates the invaluable help provided by women's support groups. In fact, the goals of such groups and the 'steps to therapy' used by many psychologists and psychiatrists often overlap and, in many cases, are identical. They typically involve for the client:

- making her feel accepted and cared for
- assuring her that she is not alone and is not to blame
- challenging the myth that violence is a normal part of intimate relationships
- offering help in motivating and facilitating changes in dealing with the violence
- identifying her own goals for immediate and long-term change
- formulating a workable plan to achieve these goals
- assessing and strengthening her commitment to carry the plan through, modifying it when necessary
- offering continuing therapeutic contact in the future, while encouraging her independence and self-development.

Women's support groups will usually discuss in a small-group setting much of the material considered in this book, such as planning safety and how men utilise violence to gain power over women. Such groups can be life-changing for many who for a long time have known nothing but craven submission and fear.

Until that course I felt I was completely alone and that no one in my situation would feel and act as I did; everything makes more sense to me now.

Helping violent men change

A number of organisations (listed at the end of the book) run programmes to try to help violent men control their abuse. These programmes will normally involve both individual and small-group work. If your partner is violent, it is worth contacting some of the help agencies for advice about how you might get him involved in their programmes. Below is an outline of what he (and you) can expect of these.

Ground rules
These constitute the general basis on which a programme runs. A typical set of rules would be:

- respect for others in the group
- active participation and involvement
- regular attendance
- honesty
- no alcohol or drugs for at least twenty-four hours before the group's meeting
- no threats or violence in the group
- confidentiality.

Contract of participation
Participants will usually have to sign an agreement to the ground rules, and penalties, such as expulsion from the group, will generally be specified for failure to meet the criteria agreed upon.

Increased self-awareness

Many men are unaware of the chain of events and signals leading up to a violent episode and fail to connect prior events with a violent act. The strategies used to heighten their self-awareness include:

- Violence checklist This is an exhaustive and highly specific list of all abusive behaviours to be avoided. The list details not only physical violence – the throwing of objects, uninvited touching, the breaking of possessions, etc. – but also other abusive behaviours: ridicule, swearing, manipulating, blaming, using pornography.
- Signals inventory The abuser compiles a personal list of signals that usually precede violence. Such signals comprise:

Trigger points Either typical areas which have led to previous violence (money, in-laws, children, etc.), or particular times of day (coming home from work) or specific places such as the bedroom.

Body language Pacing the room, pointing a finger, loss of eye contact, flailing arms, shouting, tight jaw, tension in neck or stomach.

Emotions Feeling angry, trapped, resentful, victimised, challenged, put-down, guilty, embarrassed, thwarted, foolish, unwanted.

Thoughts 'She is so stupid,' 'She is useless,' 'She always ignores me,' 'She doesn't love me,' 'She deserves a good hiding.'

- Violence log   A record of every violent episode is noted in a diary as soon as possible after the event. The triggers and signals that led up to violence are also recorded.

The purpose of increased self-awareness of the signals preceding violence is to take time out instead of lashing out.

Time out

Time out is an hour which an abuser spends away from his partner to reflect on his abusive behaviour. When the abuser recognises signs of tension building up, he calls for time out and he should calmly leave the home for **one hour** – not fifty minutes or four hours. He should not storm out and slam the door.

During this hour he should use the time in a structured way. Time out is not an excuse to disappear down to the pub for an hour. The first twenty minutes are to calm himself down. He should not drive, drink alcohol or take drugs during this time. Physical exercise such as running may help to relieve the physical tension. Alternatively, ringing up a friend who knows the situation and cares about him can be very useful. Talking relieves tension, and effective communication can often defuse violence.

The remainder of the hour should be spent going through the violence checklist and signals inventory (mentally, if he doesn't have the documents with him) and completing the violence diary. He should think about what he could have done differently and what he will say and do when he returns home. Ideally, before returning home he should ring and let his partner know that he has calmed down and is coming back. A suitable time should be found to discuss together the abuser's thoughts during the time out. If his partner does not want to talk immediately, a mutually agreeable time should be found within a day or so. If she is not prepared to talk it through at all, though, she should be left alone.

Cognitive restructuring

This is the technical term for examining why people think as they do and attempting to change the assumptions, attitudes and motivations on which such thoughts are based.

Many thought patterns may underpin abusive behaviour. Denial is invariably one of them. This serves to:

- maintain the control and power of the abuser over his partner
  - convince the abuser (and his friends and associates) that the problem isn't his
- minimise feelings of guilt and remorse in the abuser.

Denial encompasses not only refusal of responsibility for the violence and its consequences but often refusal to acknowledge the violence itself. Sometimes this is a conscious pattern of the abuser lying to himself, or sometimes he reframes his perception of some attacks.

Pushing, slapping or locking her up are not violent; only blows which cause injury constitute violence.

Denial of responsibility entails the abuser shifting the blame anywhere but on himself.

She drove me to it . . .

The stress at work made me do it , . .

It was the drink . . .

Cognitive restructuring aims to help the abuser see that every time he talks about his partner's faults when confronted with his own behaviour, he is in a state of denial. It makes him realise that he can stop the violence only once he acknowledges that he is responsible for his own actions.

Training in interpersonal skills

Abusers tend to have difficulty in defusing conflict situations even when they can recognise them at an early stage. Improving skills in conflict-reduction can be achieved by, for example, **re-enactments**. These are acted-out replays by abusers of specific recent situations which led to violence. As they role-play the incidents, their objective is to analyse what led up to the violent episodes and to identify the **critical moment** – the point at which a different response or behaviour might have prevented the violence. These alternatives are examined and then the abuser role-plays the scene again, this time with a non-violent alternative conclusion.

Relaxation training

As a build-up of tension is a major link in the chain leading to violence, the reduction of stress by means of a variety of relaxation techniques is an important feature of many programmes for violent men. Do these programmes work? Undoubtedly for some men they do.

> *I listen more now, and I know I could not have made the changes I have made without the help of the programme.*

The expectation of an instant and complete transformation from a violent man to a loving husband is not usually realistic; gradual change over time is, but the inevitable scepticism of some women's groups is sometimes justified. When attendance at such a course is a condition of a man's probation order, then there may well be cause to doubt his motivation for completing the sessions. There are also some dangers resulting from such men-only counselling and training.

- It may give you, the victim, a false sense of security about your safety.

One of my patients had a visit from her husband straight after such a course session. He wanted to tell her how well he was doing, but the evening ended up with him beating her savagely yet again.

- He may use the knowledge gained from the course to manipulate and attack you more than ever.
- He may lie to you about what takes place in the sessions.

They said that you have to have my dinner ready when I get home . . .

If you have full access to the programme materials, the potential for misuse by the abuser is minimised.

Two by two?

The suggestion that couples should receive help together to prevent further violence arouses strong feelings among experts in domestic violence. Certainly, when recent or current violence has taken place conjoint therapy is generally unwise at best and, at worst, may present further grave physical danger to the woman concerned. It is unlikely that any battered wife will feel able to respond openly and honestly to a counsellor when the man who is currently threatening her life is present in the same counselling room.

But the knee-jerk reflex that any therapy as a couple is out is probably equally unwise as an inflexible rule. Domestic violence may indeed be the man's problem, but once the violence has stopped, if the relationship is to be rebuilt, then both partners will need to come together at some point to work through the necessary process with a skilled therapist. This may be only rarely achievable but should not, in my view, be precluded universally on ideological grounds alone.

From ostriches to hawks

Once domestic violence has begun, but has not yet hardened into a relentless, repeating pattern, secondary prevention has a vital role to play. Such measures depend upon early detection, however, and for this to happen, all those involved in any aspect of children's and women's health care – nursery and play-group leaders, social workers, nurses, midwives, counsellors, teachers, hospital doctors, health visitors, CAB advisers, health educationalists and GPs – need to be aware of spouse abuse as a possible issue and be prepared to talk about it. Too many professionals bury their heads in the sand when it comes to domestic violence. If the problem is going to be tackled effectively, they must be like hawks, not ostriches.

Early detection of domestic violence involves knowing its associated features and indicators and taking a pro-active approach towards it.

Predictive signs of domestic violence
- exposure to violence in childhood either as a victim or a witness
- behavioural problems in the children – bed-wetting, truanting, stealing, etc.
- showing signs of stress at work or from unemployment
- recent major life event – childbirth, bereavement, etc
- alcohol and drug abuse

  In the abused

- low self-esteem
- sense of helplessness and dependency
- social isolation and withdrawal
- poor or non-existent social-support network
- multiple health problems

- sexual difficulties
- anxiety and depression
- recurring injuries, bruises, wounds and fractures
- reciprocal anger and aggression

In the abuser

- history of violent behaviour in general
- criminal record of use of weapons
- jealousy
- accusations of infidelity
- adverse comments to or about his partner

Taking a pro-active approach

Creating an environment in which women feel safe to talk about violence from their partners demands decisive action from both individuals and organisations alike, particularly hospitals, community clinics, counselling centres and GP surgeries. There are few good role models in this area, and any reader of this book may feel the need to take the lead. Some helpful ideas follow.

- Display posters and information leaflets in waiting-rooms to raise awareness of domestic violence and inform women of resources available to them in the local area.
- Have a place where women can talk in private with staff.
- Maintain strict standards of confidentiality at all times.
- Ask about violence as a routine part of client assessment. I find that violence in the family is quite a common problem these days and I often ask about it as a matter of routine. Have you ever experienced a relationship in which you were hit, threatened, hurt or felt afraid in any way?
- Raise the issue of violence in conversation with others. On many occasions when I have done this it has led to their

opening up about either personal experience of violence or clients, friends or neighbours who have experienced it.

Even in an environment which gives women permission and active encouragement to talk about their abuse, many will initially keep silent because of society's strong taboos about domestic violence as a whole. Nevertheless they recognise a safe haven when they see it and will be able to return with confidence maybe many months later.

Turning the tide

Primary prevention of domestic violence involves changing social mores and attitudes through education and public-awareness campaigns. In Britain in 1993 the Government launched a strong and effective national advertising campaign to highlight awareness of domestic violence. One poster depicted three well-dressed, respectable-looking male professionals under the banner headline 'Behind these successful men are the women they put in casualty'. The punchline on every poster ran: 'Domestic violence. It's not just a fact of life. It's a crime.'

It would be naïve and foolish to expect that such campaigns will in themselves deter wife-batterers. The cultural and psychological factors that initiate and maintain such behaviour are not likely to be altered significantly by impersonal media messages. But such messages do help to redefine and draw attention to the problem in the public consciousness; they also help to link abused women with the very services that may be able to help them.

Of course, increased public consciousness may have its dangers, such as the more frequent reporting of cases that turn out to be unfounded or the raising of expectations of help which cannot be matched by the local resources, thus intensifying the pain of victimisation. Overall, though, the heightening of awareness of domestic violence as a major social issue is necessary if resources are ever to be committed seriously to other aspects of primary prevention such as:

- the reduction of social isolation and incorporation of families into a meaningful community network
- the reduction of the social stresses such as poverty and inequality of worth, which provoke violence
- the countering of social norms that legitimise or even glorify violence, such as the use of violence as a form of media entertainment
- the changing of the sexist character of education, including teaching on violence as part of the educational curriculum.

If the cycle of repetition of domestic violence through the generations is to be interrupted, helping children to choose alternative strategies to violence is essential. Parental example, as we have seen, is vitally important. However, for the increasing number of children whose home life involves witnessing a continual round of arguments and fights between parents, the inclusion of domestic violence in the school syllabus may provide the only opportunity they have to discuss their problems. Despite this crying need, very few schools include any discussion of domestic violence in their personal, health and social-education timetable. The research data on the effects of school prevention programmes is very sparse.

One study from Ontario, Canada, shows some hopeful signs, however.[1] Four high schools participated by giving a half or a whole day to the topic of domestic violence. A whole-school presentation, using videos on wife assault and a talk by a survivor, was followed by small-group discussion work facilitated by professionals experienced in handling domestic-violence issues.

Students were given a questionnaire to complete before, immediately after and six weeks after the presentation in the school. The questionnaire sought to detect changes in the students' knowledge of, attitudes towards and future behavioural intentions about domestic violence. Significant positive changes were reported for girls, but for boys there were as many changes in a negative as in a positive direction. The authors of the study suggest that many of the boys whose sexist and violent attitudes were apparently worsened by the programme may have already been involved in violence towards their girlfriends and that intervention should be targeted at a lower age than that of high-school students.

In Britain 'Lives in Your Hands' is a remarkably successful course run in Leeds by Ruth Hanson, a research psychologist with special interests in criminology and child abuse. This course is not school-based but for homeless young men who have been abused themselves and are living in hostels run by local Christian charities. The course looks at childhood development and how to deal with children, and it runs for an evening each week for eight weeks. The course outline states that 'although designed for the anti-authority, cynical, low-in-self-esteem, illiterate young man "Lives in Your Hands" invariably draws the comment that "all young people should have this course."'[2]

Though designed primarily to help prevent men from abusing children, one of the effects noted in those who had attended the course was that they also treated their girlfriends and the women staffworkers with much greater respect. If such a positive effect in the treatment of women could be obtained with such 'hard cases', what could be achieved with a similar programme in ordinary schools? It is in part because women are not respected that they are battered.

Some twenty-five years ago, Kitty Genovese was beaten to death by a man in a New York street in full view of more than a hundred people. No one helped her. Not a single person intervened, shouted at her assailant to stop or even made a simple phone call to the police – until she was dead, that is. When the police eventually arrived, they asked many of these witnesses why they did nothing. The most common answer was not, 'I was afraid I might get hurt,' 'I thought someone else would do it,' or even 'I didn't think it was any of my business.' It was, 'I thought they were married.'[3]

Has much changed in twenty-five years? Similar thoughts and the attitudes behind them still fertilise the growth of domestic violence – the abuse, the battering and, ultimately, the killing of women. Their lives are in all our hands. In schools, colleges and universities, in work-places and places of worship, in council chambers and national governments, in clinics, surgeries and hospitals, and not least as individuals, we need to respond. What will we do to help them?

Notes

Preface

1 J. Mooney, *The Hidden Figures: Domestic Violence in North London*, Islington Council, Centre for Criminology, Middlesex University, 1993.
2 R. Dobash and R. Dobash, *Violence Against Wives*, Open Books, 1980.

Chapter 1: Home is Where the Hurt Hides

1 L. Dickstein, 'Spouse Abuse and Other Domestic Violence', *Psychiatr. Clin. North Am.*, vol. 11, no. 4, 1988, pp. 611–28.
2 British Crime Survey, 1992.
3 A. Flitcraft, S. Hadley *et al.*, *Diagnostic and Treatment Guidelines on Domestic Violence*, American Medical Association, 1992.
4 G. Hotaling, D. Finkelhor *et al.*, *Family Abuse and Its Consequences*, Sage, 1989.
5 J. Mooney, *The Hidden Figures: Domestic Violence in North London*, Islington Council, Centre for Criminology, Middlesex University, 1993.

6 R. Hall, *Ask Any Woman*, Falling Wall Press, 1985; D. Russell, *Rape in Marriage*, Macmillan, 1982.
7 Crime Statistics (England and Wales), 1993.

Chapter 2: Prone to Violence

1 R. Gelles, 'Violence in the Family', *Journal of Marriage*, vol. 42, 1980, pp. 873–85.
2 G. Hotaling and D. Sugarman, 'An Analysis of Risk Markers in Husband to Wife Violence: the Current State of Knowledge', *Violence and Victims*, vol. 1, no. 2, 1982, pp. 101–24.
3 Quoted on the front cover of the first edition of R. Meadow, *ABC of Child Abuse*, BMJ, 1989. When the second edition was published in 1993 the quotation was removed; presumably by then it was thought politically incorrect.
4 J. Gayford, 'Domestic Violence' in J. Shepherd (ed.), *Violence in Healthcare*, OUP, 1994.
5 H. Schlute, M. Hall *et al.*, 'Domestic Violence Associated with Anabolic Steroid Abuse', *Am. J. Psychiat.*, vol. 150, no. 2, 1993, p. 348.
6 Quoted in J. Babcock, J. Waltz *et al.*, 'Power and Violence: the Relationship Between Communication Patterns, Power Discrepancies and Domestic Violence', *Journal of Consulting and Clinical Psychology*, vol. 61, 1993, pp. 40–50.
7 Quoted in P. Schaff (ed.), *Works of Chrysostom*, New York, 1889.
8 Thomas Aquinas, *Summa Theologiae*, vol. 1, 92.1.
9 J. Drane and O. Drane, *Happy Families?*, HarperCollins, 1995.
10 J. Alsdurf and P. Alsdurf, *Battered Into Submission*, Highland, 1990.
11 The Koran, trs. N. J. Dawood, Penguin Books, 1995 edn, 4:34.

12 K. Yllo, 'The Status of Women, Marital Equality and Violence Against Wives', *Journal of Family Issues*, vol. 5, no. 3, 1984, p. 312.

13 A. Jones and S. Schechter, *When Love Goes Wrong*, Gollancz, 1992.

14 L. Walker, *The Battered Woman*, Harper & Row, 1979; *The Hidden Victims: Children and Domestic Violence*, NCH Action for Children, 1994.

15 Dr Liz Kelly in a paper presented at 'Domestic Violence: the Victim and the Perpetrator', a conference at St George's Hospital Medical School, London, on 18 October 1995.

16 R. Whelan, *Broken Homes and Battered Children*, Family Education Trust, 1994.

17 K. Yllo and M. Straus, 'Interpersonal Violence Among Married and Cohabiting Couples', *Family Relations*, vol. 30, 1981, pp. 339–47.

18 K. D. O'Leary, J. Malone *et al.*, 'Physical Aggression in Early Marriage: Pre-relationship and Relationship Effects', *Journal of Consulting and Clinical Psychology*, vol. 62, 1994, pp. 594–602.

19 M. Daly, L. Singh *et al.*, 'Children Fathered by Previous Partners: a Risk Factor for Violence Against Women', *Canadian Journal of Public Health*, vol. 84, 1993, pp. 209–10.

20 E. Sommers and J. Check, 'An Empirical Investigation of the Role of Pornography in the Verbal and Physical Abuse of Women', *Violence and Victims*, vol. 2, 1987, pp. 189–209.

21 E. Cramer and J. McFarlane, 'Pornography and the Abuse of Women', *Public Health Nursing*, vol. 11, 1994, pp. 268–72.

22 P. Tournier, *The Violence Within*, Harper & Row, 1978.

Chapter 3: Battered Into Submission

1 L. Walker, *The Battered Woman Syndrome*, Springer, 1984.
2 M. Pagelow, 'Marital Rape' in V. Van Hassalt, A. Morrison *et al.* (eds.), *Handbook of Family Violence*, Plenum, 1988.
3 A. Gielen, P. O'Campo, 'Interpersonal Conflict and Physical Violence During the Childbearing Year', *Soc. Sci. Med.*, vol. 39, 1994, pp. 781–7.

Chapter 4: Coming Back for More

1 L. Walker, *The Battered Woman Syndrome*, Springer, 1984.
2 Quoted in N. Dougherty, 'Female Masochism: Perspectives for Social Workers', *Clinical Social Work Journal*, vol. 15, no. 1, 1987, pp. 22–34.
3 J. Gayford, 'Ten Types of Battered Wives', *Welfare Officer*, vol. 25, 19xx, pp. 5–9.
4 Malachi 2:16, Holy Bible: New International Version, Hodder & Stoughton, 1973.
5 Summarised in J. Burgoyne *et al.*, *Divorce Matters*, Penguin Books, 1987, and J. Tripp, M. Cockett *et al.*, *The Exeter Report*, Department of Child Health, University of Exeter, 1994.

Chapter 5: Not in Front of the Children

1 *The Hidden Victims: Children and Domestic Violence*, NCH Action for Children, 1994.
2 M. Straus, R. Gelles *et al.*, *Behind Closed Doors: Violence in the American Family*, Anchor, 1980.
3 Crime Statistics (England and Wales), 1993.
4 D. Black and T. Kaplan, 'Father Kills Mother', *British Journal of Psychiatry*, vol. 153, 1988, pp. 624–30.
5 R. Pynoos and S. Eth, 'The Child as Witness to

Homicide', *Journal of Social Issues*, vol. 40, no. 2, 1984, pp. 87–108.

Chapter 6: Survival Tactics

1 *Minneapolis Star and Tribune*, 18 August 1986.
2 T. Stammers, *The Family Guide to Sex and Intimacy*, Hodder & Stoughton, 1994.

Chapter 7: Take It Like a Man

1 M. Pagelow, 'Adult Victims of Domestic Violence', *Journal of Interpersonal Violence*, vol. 7, 1992, pp. 87–120.
2 S. Smith, D. Buchan *et al.*, 'Adult Domestic Violence', *Health Trends*, vol. 24, 1992, pp. 97–9.
3 Pagelow, 'Adult Victims of Domestic Violence'.
4 L. Brinkworth, 'What Makes a Woman Hit a Man?', *Cosmopolitan*, February 1995.
5 *Wimbledon Guardian*, 11 May 1994.
6 Brinkworth, 'What Makes a Woman Hit a Man?'.
7 Quoted in J. Hammond, 'I was a Battered Husband', magazine cutting, source unknown.
8 Quoted in D. Thomas, *Not Guilty: Men – The Case for the Defence*, Weidenfeld & Nicolson, 1993.
9 A. Kirsta, *Deadlier Than the Male*, HarperCollins, 1994.

Chapter 8: An End to the Raging

1 P. Jaffe, M. Sudermann *et al.*, 'An Evaluation of a Secondary-school Primary Prevention Programme on Violence in Intimate Relationships', *Violence and Victims*, vol. 7, 1992, pp. 129–46.
2 Obtainable from Ruth Hanson, Outwood House, Outwood Lane, Leeds LS18 4HR.

3 C. Esposito, 'Abuse: Breaking the Cycle of Violence', *Trends in Health Care, Law and Ethics*, vol. 8, 1993, pp. 7–11.

Support Agencies and Helpline Contacts

Violence and abuse

For women

Bhavan (safe housing for Asian women)	0181 640 6296
Chinese Women Refuge Group Instrument House, 209–15 King's Cross Rd, London WC1 9DB	0171 837 7297
Chinese Women's Domestic Violence Hotline	0171 494 3861
Chiswick Family Rescue PO Box 855, London W4 4JF	0171 747 0133 24-hour line 0171 995 4430
Domestic Violence Intervention Project PO Box 2838, London W6 9ZE	0181 748 6512
Irish Women's Domestic Violence Project PO Box 4662, London SE23 2UT	0171 251 6537 Mobile 0956 507096
London Rape Crisis PO Box 69, London WC1X 9NJ	0171 837 1600

London Women's Aid   0171 251 6537
52–4 Featherstone St, London EC1Y 8RT

National Women's Aid Federation
   England: 0117 963 3542
PO Box 391, Bristol BS99 7WS
   N. Ireland: 01232 249 041
129 University St, Belfast, BT7 1HP   or 249 538
   Scotland: 0131 221 0401
12 Torphichen St, Edinburgh EH3 8JQ   or 229 1419
   Wales: 01222 390 874
38–48 Crwys Rd, Cardiff CF2 4NN

Southall Black Sisters (helpline for Asian   0181 571 9595
and black women)

For men
CHANGE Project   01786 67745
University of Stirling, Stirling SK9 4LA

Domestic Violence Intervention Project   0181 563 7983
PO Box 2838, London W6 9ZE

Everyman   0181 793 0155
30A Brixton Rd, Kennington,
London SW9 6BU

Merton Male   0181 543 1102
PO Box 402, Sutton SM1 3TG

General support and advicelines

Association of Christian Counsellers,   01735 662207
175 Wokingham Rd, Reading RG6 1LU

British Association of Counselling   01788 578328
1 Regent Place, Rugby CV21 2PJ

Care for the Family,   0222 497807
136 Newport Rd, Cardiff CF2 1DF

Childline   Freephone 0800 1111
Freepost 1111, London EC4 4BB

Criminal Injuries Compensation Board   0171 936 3476
Morley House, Holborn Viaduct,
London EC1A 2JQ

National Council for One-Parent Families   0171 267 1361
255 Kentish Town Rd, London NW5 2LX

National Family Conciliation Council   01739 514 055
Shaftesbury Centre, Percy St,
Swindon SW2 2AZ

National Society for the Prevention of   0171 242 1626
Cruelty to Children
67, Saffron Hill, London EC1N 8RS

Relate   01788 573 241
Herbert Gray College, Little Church St,
Rugby CV21 3AP

Victim Support   0171 735 9166
Cranmer House, 39 Brixton Rd,
London SW9 6DZ

Alcohol and drug addiction

Adfam   0171 638 3700
5th Floor, Epworth House, 35 City Rd,
London EC1Y 1AA

Alcoholics Anonymous   01904 644026 and
PO Box 1, Stonebow House, Stonebow,   0171 352 3001
York Y01 2NJ

Al-Anon Family Groups   0171 403 0888
61 Great Dover St, London SE1 4YF

Families Anonymous   0171 281 8889
650 Holloway Rd, London N19 3NV

Narcotics Anonymous   0171 351 6794
PO Box 1980, London N19 3LS

Support agencies in USA

Centre for the Prevention of Sexual and   206 634 1903
Domestic Violence
1914 North Thirty Forth St, Suite 105,
Seattle WA 98103-9058

Child Help National Child Abuse Hotline   1 800 422 4453
PO Box 630, Hollywood CA 90028

Family Violence and Sexual Assault   903 595 6600
Institute
1310 Clinic Drive, Tyler TX 75701

National Association for Children of   301 468 0985
Alcoholics
11426 Rockville Pike, Suite 100,
Rockville MD 20852

National Council on Child Abuse and   202 429 6695
Family Violence
1155 Connecticut Ave NW,
Washington DC 20036

National Domestic Violence Hotline   1 800 333 7233

National Victim Centre   817 877 3355
309 West Seventh Street, Suite 705,
Fort Worth TX 76102

Support agencies in Australia

New South Wales
Domestic Violence Advocacy Service   02 637 3741
Women's Refuge Resource Centre   02 560 1605

24-hour Refuge Referral Service	02 799 6949

Northern Territory
Darwin Crisis Line	089 81 9227

Queensland
Aboriginal Women's Group	07 844 1146
24-hour Crisis Care	07 227 5999
Domestic Violence Resource Centre	07 857 6299
Migrant Women's Emergency Support	07 846 3490
Women's Infolink	07 229 1264

Victoria
Domestic Violence Resource Centre	03 387 9155
Women's Refuge Referral Service	03 329 8525
Women's Information and Referral Exchange	03 654 6844

Western Australia
24-hour Crisis Care Unit	09 325 1111 or 008 199 008
Women's Refuge Group	09 325 7220
Multicultural	09 325 7716
Women's Information and Referral Exchange	008 199 174

Tasmania
24-hour Crisis Intervention Units
Burnie	004 34 6212 Day 004 34 6230 Night
Launceston	003 36 2379 Day 003 32 3101 Night
Hobart	002 33 2529